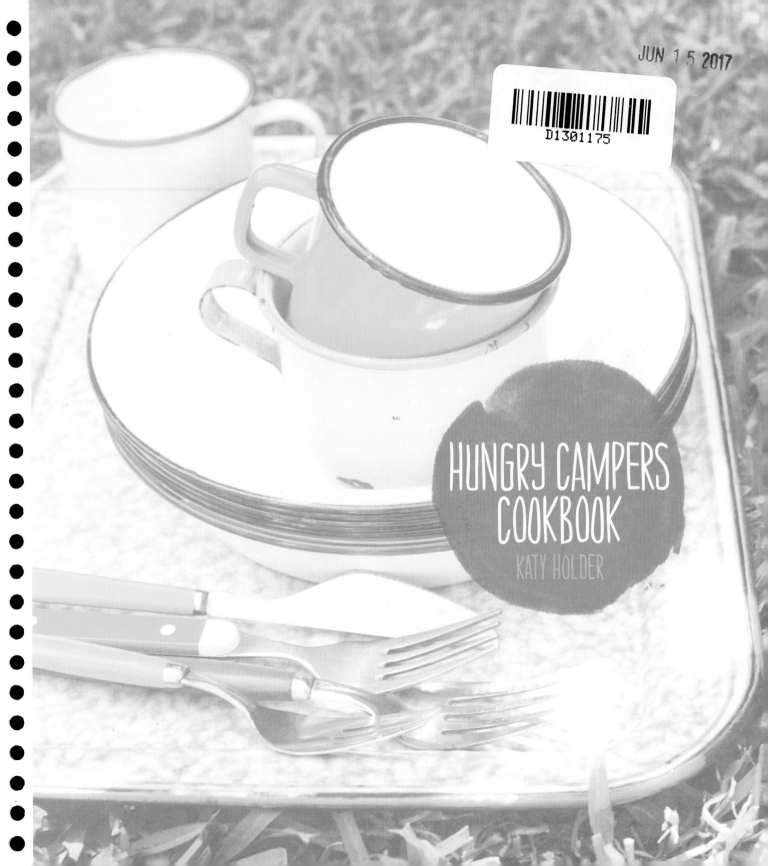

HUNGRY CAMPERS
COOKBOOK
KATY HOLDER

HUNGRY CAMPERS COOKBOOK

Fresh, healthy and easy recipes to cook on your next camping trip

hardie grant books

KATY HOLDER

This book is dedicated to
my own big and little hungry
campers, Alex, Max and Jack.

Thanks for munching your way
through this book and for so
many fun camping adventures.

CONTENTS

INTRODUCTION viii

MAKE AT HOME SNACKS
xviii

PREPARE AHEAD MEALS
16

CATCH OF THE DAY
36

FIRE UP THE BARBECUE
50

ONE-POT DINNERS
68

SALADS, BIG AND SMALL
90

CAMPFIRE COOKING FOR KIDS
122

CAMPFIRE BREAD AND OTHER ESSENTIALS
142

DELICIOUS ENDINGS
156

INDEX 168
ACKNOWLEDGEMENTS 173

INTRODUCTION

My camping 'career' started at age six, when I camped out in the back garden of our London home during the summer holidays. I was so excited to put up my tiny orange ridge tent, light a small fire and heat up some beans and bake a few potatoes. Snuggled down in my sleeping bag, reading by the light of a torch seemed like the ultimate adventure and I haven't looked back since.

We progressed to family camping holidays every summer, where my siblings and I revelled in the freedom the campsite gave us. As an adult, I have camped all over the world and have now introduced my love of camping to my two sons – fortunately my husband was already a fan. We always travel to our campsite by car and this book has been written with this in mind, as it allows us to carry additional utensils and equipment to make our trips a little easier and more luxurious.

The *Hungry Campers Cookbook* is for everyone who goes camping, or aspires to go camping, and who wants to eat delicious camp-made food. Every recipe has been cooked at a campsite far from home but will also work in a domestic kitchen. With a little forethought and preparation, eating under the stars can be as good, if not better, than any meal eaten at home.

Katy Holder

Camping as a child, 1975

PACKING YOUR COOLER

One of the biggest joys of camping is that it allows you to get back to basics and live a simple lifestyle for a while. The drawback of this, however, is that you can't just reach into the refrigerator when you want cheese for your sandwich or an ice cold beer. Plus, you need to give careful consideration to how you will store your food to prevent it going off. The cooler that you use for drinks at your Sunday afternoon barbecue isn't going to cut it for a three- or four-day camping trip, as the walls aren't sufficiently insulated. Invest in a proper cooler, and ice packs, which are all available from a camping or outdoor store.

Giving a little consideration to how you pack your chilled food before you go will not only help to keep your food cold, but also make finding things and keeping them in good condition easier.

- Freeze any milk, juice and bottles of water you're going to take with you – these will double as ice packs and defrost over the first day or two.

- Freeze packets of bacon, sausages and meat before you leave. Not only does this make them last longer without going off, but the frozen packets also act as additional ice packs.

- Put any snacks or meals you are preparing in advance (*see* chapters 1 and 2), into airtight containers, then freeze the meals. Takeaway containers work well for this and can be stacked neatly in your cooler – they will also do a similar job to an ice pack for the journey. Don't forget to remove the one you want to eat for dinner so it defrosts in time!

- Pack cheeses into shallow storage containers to prevent them getting squashed. Do the same with packets of meat. Keep things well wrapped to prevent cross-contamination.

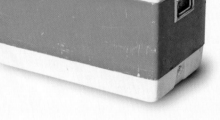

- Many butchers will vacuum pack meat for a small charge, so ask about this when buying your meat. Although the meat will still need to be stored in a cooler, it should last for an extra three to four days longer than un-sealed meats. If you have some fresh meat that isn't going to last another day, cook it then chill it and eat it the next day for lunch.

- Use good-quality ice packs and leave room at the top of your cool box for a layer of them, as the cold air will sink down.

PACKING NON-PERISHABLE FOODS

Packing all of the items not stored inside your cooler also requires a little forethought and planning, as space at the campsite is often at a premium. You can also save yourself a lot of time and energy when you arrive, if you keep in mind the following tips.

- Save a storage container of small packets of tomato ketchup, soy sauce, sugar, salt and other condiments that often come with takeaway meals for taking on weekend and shorter camping trips. For longer trips, it's better to take regular bottles and jars as there is less packaging to dispose of.

- Write the contents on the top of your containers using a washable marker, as more often than not you'll be rummaging in boxes to find things and the lid will be the easiest to spot. Stick white labels on the tops of spice jars to easily spot them in your food stocks.

- Think about decanting some ingredients into smaller containers before you leave home, based on how long you will be away and how many people you will need to feed. If you think you are going to make pancakes one morning, weigh out the flour and baking powder and put into an airtight container or re-sealable snack bag and label it so when you get to the campsite you know exactly what it's for. Then all you have to do is add your milk and eggs and you're ready to cook.

- Although you could take a bottle of store-bought salad dressing, think about mixing some up before you go. If you don't use it all on your trip, it keeps well and you can always use it up at home. At its simplest, a dressing is just a combination of olive oil and vinegar – one part vinegar to two or three parts oil and some salt and pepper. Throw in a peeled garlic clove and a teaspoon of mustard if you like.

Note on measurements: *This book uses metric cup measurements, i.e. 250 ml for 1 cup; in the US a cup is 8 fl oz, just smaller, and American cooks should be generous in their cup measurements. This book also uses 15 ml (½ fl oz) tablespoons; cooks with 20 ml (¾ fl oz) tablespoons should be scant with their tablespoon measurements.*

ESSENTIAL FOOD ITEMS

Some of the recipes in this book include a 'don't forget' tip to ensure you have all of the ingredients you need for the recipe to taste as good as it should. This usually relates to store cupboard ingredients that might be forgotten in a last-minute packing frenzy. When you're camping out in the wilderness you can't just pop out to the corner shop – there's nothing worse than starting to cook a recipe and realising you've forgotten an important ingredient. Here, I've suggested items that I usually pack. I don't have dedicated food for camping, instead I take from my kitchen cupboards so I know it's fresh.

BUTTER I take a spreadable butter in a tub rather than the blocks wrapped in paper as it stores more efficiently and is less likely to be found melted at the bottom of the cooler.

BREAD, ROLLS AND PITA POCKETS Good to use for breakfast toast, to make sandwiches for lunches, to mop up curries and stews or to make pizza calzone (page 126) or any of the kebabs.

BREAKFAST SPREADS Marmalade, jam, peanut butter and honey. Also useful to have if you make breakfast pancakes (page 124).

CAPERS AND OLIVES These two ingredients can instantly transform a recipe. I love them in salads, pasta sauces and dressings.

CEREALS As a general rule, I am opposed to eating sugary breakfast cereals, however, as a treat and for convenience every few camping trips I buy the selection packs or mini cereals available at most supermarkets. Not only do the kids love this treat, but I have an ulterior

motive – less washing up! I open the boxes and plastic inserts carefully at the top, then pour the milk straight in. The kids love the fun aspect of it and all that's left to wash up is a spoon.

CHEESE Pack a variety. I usually buy some pre-sliced to make preparing sandwiches easy and then a bag of grated cheese for using on pasta and pizza. And don't forget the decadent wheel of brie or camembert for the camp-fired warmed cheese (page 162).

CHUTNEY Great for a quick baste or marinade, chutney elevates a humble sandwich to something more special.

COLD MEATS Pack a selection of sliced ham, salami and chicken – as well as sandwich fillings, they can be used for pizzas and tortilla roll-ups (page 125).

CONDIMENTS Pack ketchup, mayonnaise, pasta or pizza sauce. Either bring those you have in your fridge, or if buying specifically for your trip, buy smaller bottles or jars that take up less space.

HERBS The best way to transport and store fresh herbs for a camping trip is to prepare and pack them before you leave home. Rinse them under cold water, then shake off any excess and wrap in damp paper towel. Place in a small airtight container and store in the refrigerator until you set off, then store in your cooler until needed.

MILK Many campers take long-life milk with them. I prefer freezing fresh milk before I go to ensure it lasts longer. Buy bottles with lids rather than a carton if you can, to prevent leakage in your cooler.

OIL Only take one oil to save space and use it for everything – frying, marinades, bastes and dressings.

PESTO Ideal for quick pasta sauces, using in marinades and stirring into soups. For camping, I'm happy with a good quality store-bought jar of pesto, but by all means make your own before you leave if you like.

SALAD INGREDIENTS Preventing salad leaves from getting squashed is an ongoing issue for me! Take whole lettuces and pack them at the top of you cooler, or take pre-packed boxes, wash the leaves before you go and pack them in airtight containers with a layer of damp paper towel in the bottom to keep the leaves fresh. Store in the cooler.

SALT AND PEPPER I take a small container of sea salt (labelled on the top) and one of those plastic pepper grinders available in the spice racks at supermarkets.

SPICES I always take the basic flavourings, which for me include ground cumin, ground coriander, paprika or chilli powder. They quickly add extra flavour to stews, marinades, soups and salad dressings.

SUGAR If you take sugar in your tea or coffee you won't need a whole bag, so decant some into a small jar. Clearly label this so you don't get it confused with salt!

TEA, COFFEE AND HOT CHOCOLATE We love good coffee and just because you're camping it doesn't mean you need to resort to instant coffee from a jar. Take either a plunger or stovetop espresso maker, which you can place over the fire. Hot chocolate is ideal for cool winter mornings and early evenings.

VINEGARS Pack your favourite vinegar for salad dressings. Balsamic or white wine vinegar would be my choice.

WATER Some campsites, particularly the more remote ones, don't have running water available. Check before you go. Often they are by a river where you can wash and get water for washing up, but you'll need to take all your water for drinking and cooking. Buy a couple of 25-litre water containers and fill them at home before you leave. Keep them in the shade when you are at the campsite so they remain cool for drinking.

WHAT COOKING UTENSILS SHOULD I TAKE?

Many campers keep boxes of utensils in the shed specifically for camping. Although I do have a set of crockery just for this purpose, I find it easier to simply decide what I'm cooking then take the necessary utensils from my drawers.

As well as the items listed below, you'll also need cutlery, crockery, cups and glasses for everyone. When my kids were small, I used those plates that have separate compartments. I found these easier as they tend to have a lip around the edge, so if you're eating sitting in a chair rather than at the table, less food falls off.

BOWLS   One large metal or plastic bowl for mixing and serving salads, a medium-sized bowl and a couple of small bowls for making marinades and dressings. I also take a large plastic bowl or tub for washing up – look for eco-friendly washing up liquid in camping stores and keep it with your camping equipment.

CHOPPING BOARDS   Take one or two plastic chopping boards.

KNIVES   Take one small and one medium sharp knife and a bread knife if you're not taking sliced bread.

LIGHTER   A gas stove lighter is more reliable and safer than matches, although waterproof matches are handy to have around.

PANS   Bring a frying pan, a medium saucepan and a small saucepan.

PEELER   As water can often be scarce, peeling is easier than washing many vegetables and fruits.

SIEVE   I found a collapsible sieve at a camping store. It packs flat, so now it comes on every trip.

SKEWERS   Wooden or metal, but remember to soak wooden skewers beforehand to prevent them burning during cooking.

SPADE   Not strictly cooking equipment, but necessary if cooking using coals as you'll need to move the coals around.

SPOONS   Take a couple of large spoons, metal or plastic for serving and stirring.

TEA TOWELS   For washing up and handling hot pans, or you might prefer an ovenproof mit for cooking around the fire.

CAN OPENER   And don't forget the bottle opener too!

TONGS   Handy not only for the barbecue but also for tossing salads.

FLASHLIGHT   Although not strictly cooking equipment, keep your flashlight or headlamp at hand while cooking at night.

INVEST IN A CAMP OVEN

If you camp a lot then a camp oven, or Dutch oven, is a very worthwhile investment. A camp oven is a cast-iron casserole dish that can be used for all your one-pot meals that are cooked over a fire, including stews, soups, breads and desserts. If you don't have a camp oven you could use something similar like a Le Creuset. However, be aware as it will probably blacken over the heat. Ensure any dish you use is suitable for an open heat source.

It is not advisable to use a camp oven on a gas cooker. As I see it, a camp oven works almost like your home oven, creating heat all around the food, achieved by putting coals around and on top. You cannot achieve the same effect with gas. Keep your camp oven for cooking over an open fire and use saucepans over gas.

Your camp oven may need seasoning when you first buy it, so check the manufacturer's instructions. This is done to remove any coating that was applied during manufacture. Your camp oven will also need a bit of love and care after each use, but it's worth it. Once you've served up all the food, put a little bit of water into the dish, put the lid on and sit it close to the fire to warm through (you can always do this while you're eating). Ensure the water isn't too hot, then wipe out any food scraps. Don't use any detergents on your oven (unless you have had it for years and it is very well seasoned). Dry the pot well, preferably sitting it by the fire or use a tea towel, then re-season by coating the insides, including the lid, with cooking oil to prevent it rusting – this is easiest done with paper towel. Wipe off any excess oil.

This really isn't as much of a hassle as it sounds. After your tent, sleeping bag and mattress, this is one of the most useful pieces of camping equipment you can have.

COOKING OVER AN OPEN FIRE

There are a variety of ways to cook your food when you are camping – over an open fire, using a gas cooker or cooking on a barbecue. Where possible, my preference is to cook over an open fire. However, we also always take our two-gas burner for boiling water and making breakfast, as during the summer months we don't light a fire first thing in the morning and of course, sometimes you can't have fires at all when fire bans are in place.

All the recipes in this book can be cooked over any heat source, with the exception of the slow-cooked one-pot meals, which really do work best over a fire. Although you can slow-cook over gas, you cannot use your camp oven effectively over gas. Also, if you are at a campsite with shared coking facilities, cooking something for two hours might be considered a little antisocial!

When cooking over an open fire the most important consideration is to ensure a regular temperature, that is neither too hot or too cool. Don't cook over large flames, start the fire an hour or so ahead of when you want to cook, so that you have got hot coals to provide a more constant heat source. If you have an open fire, you can either put a grill rack over the fire and cook on this, or for many of the one-pot meals and when baking bread, I sit a camp oven on the ground, then surround it with coals, shifting them with a spade. I also then put coals on the lid of the camp oven, replacing them periodically to ensure constant heat. It's not advisable to sit the camp oven directly on the coals as you will probably burn the bottom of your food.

If you are cooking over a fire in a fire pit or ring, there is often a grill plate that swings around so you can cook your food on this. Alternatively, clear a space in the ring and cook directly on the ground.

Keep in mind that cooking times will vary depending on the cut of meat or ingredient you are cooking (for example, a thick cut of meat will take longer to cook than thin); the heat of your fire and whether it's windy or not when you barbecue. Don't worry, all of the recipes in this book are pretty forgiving of temperature variations.

MAKE AT HOME SNACKS

Just being in the outdoors, even if you're not running around with the kids, can increase your appetite. To satisfy cravings, ravenous campers often turn to unhealthy supermarket snacks, such as chips and chocolate. Whenever we go camping, I take the time to prepare a few treats in advance — homemade snacks taste just as delicious, but have the added bonus of filling you up without the preservatives. These offerings are great for passing around the back seat during long car trips, although I also keep some separate to enjoy when we arrive.

Banana and coconut bread lasts for several days and can be quickly toasted in a frying pan or over the fire for a new lease on life. With recipes for cookies, granola bars and scrumptious brownies, you're all set for when a troupe of campers looking for an energy boost chorus 'I'm hungry!'

BANANA AND COCONUT BREAD

We nearly always take a loaf of this banana bread with us on camping trips. It's quick to prepare and there's always enough to feed a crowd. Any that isn't eaten on the day you bake it can be toasted briefly in a pan or over the fire and served warm, spread with a little butter.

MAKES 1 loaf

3 ripe bananas, mashed well
2 eggs, lightly beaten
150 g (1¼ cup) all-purpose flour
100 g (1 cup) shredded coconut
180 g (1 cup) sugar
1 teaspoon salt
1 teaspoon baking soda

1 Preheat a conventional oven to 200°C (400°F/Gas 4). Grease and line the base and sides of a 21 x 11 cm (8 x 4 in) loaf (bar) tin or other similar tin with baking paper.

2 Put the mashed banana in a large bowl and mix in the eggs; it's quicker if you use electric beaters, but not essential. One by one, beat in the flour, then the coconut, sugar, salt and baking soda until combined.

3 Spoon the mixture into the prepared tin and bake for about 50 minutes. If the top starts to brown too much, cover with foil for the remaining cooking time. To ensure the loaf is cooked, stick a skewer into the loaf and leave for 5 seconds before removing – if it comes out dry it is cooked.

4 Remove the bread from the oven and allow to cool in the tin for 5 minutes, before turning out onto a wire rack to cool completely.

5 Serve the banana bread warm or at room temperature, cut into slices.

HOMEMADE FRUIT AND NUT GRANOLA BARS

Pack a few pieces of this nutritious slice for long car journeys or if you're going on a hike. They are ideal for hungry tummies after a day at the beach or to break up a lazy afternoon. I suggest making large squares, but they can also be cut smaller for a quick bite if you prefer.

MAKES about 15 pieces

90 g (¼ cup) honey
100 g (½ cup) butter
**100 g (½ cup lightly packed)
  soft brown sugar**
200 g (2 cups) rolled oats
**40 g (⅓ cup) chopped
  hazelnuts**
**40 g (⅓ cup) chopped
  walnuts or pistachios**
**120 g (¾ cup) mixed dried
  fruit, such as raisins,
  apricots, cranberries,
  dates and sultanas
  (golden raisins), larger
  pieces diced**

1 Preheat a conventional oven to 190°C (375°F/Gas 3). Line a shallow 26 x 17 cm (11 x 7 in) baking tin or other similar tin with parchment paper.

2 Put the honey, butter and sugar in a saucepan over low heat. Melt the butter slowly, stirring occasionally to combine. Do not boil. Remove from the heat and stir well.

3 In a separate bowl, combine the oats, nuts and fruit. Add to the honey mixture, stirring well to ensure the dry ingredients are coated. Spoon the mixture into the prepared tin and use the back of a large spoon or spatula to press it down into the edges and smooth the top. Bake for about 30 minutes – the slice should be dark golden.

4 Remove from the oven and leave to cool in the tin for 10 minutes, then cut the slice into about 15 pieces. Leave to cool completely in the tin, then re-cut the slice when cool and store in an airtight container for up to four days.

If you don't want to include nuts, just add an extra 80 g (⅔ cup) dried fruit.

OAT AND RAISIN COOKIES

These rustic, quick-to-prepare cookies can be baked on the morning of your camping trip or the night before. They can be stored for up to four days in an airtight container, although they may not last that long! This recipe can be doubled to make more if you are cooking for a crowd.

MAKES about 20 cookies

75 g (½ cup) whole wheat flour
150 g (1½ cups) rolled oats
1 teaspoon baking powder
30 g (¼ cup) chopped hazelnuts or walnuts
80 g (½ cup) raisins
60 g (¼ cup) butter, at room temperature
115 g (⅓ cup) honey
1 egg, lightly beaten
1 teaspoon natural vanilla extract

1 Combine the flour, oats, baking powder, nuts and raisins in a large bowl.

2 In a separate bowl, beat together the butter, honey, egg and vanilla extract for 1–2 minutes using electric beaters. Using a spoon, stir in the dry ingredients and mix well until thoroughly combined.

3 Transfer the mixture to the refrigerator for 30 minutes to harden slightly. If you are running short of time, you can skip this step, but the cookies will hold their shape and have a better texture if you refrigerate the dough first.

4 Preheat the oven to 170°C (340°F/Gas 3). Line two parchment trays with parchment paper. Using about 1 tablespoon of the mixture at a time, roll into balls, then place onto the prepared trays about 3 cm (1¼ in) apart – press down gently on each cookie so they are about 5 mm (about ¼ in) thick. Bake in the oven for 12–15 minutes, or until lightly golden.

5 Remove the cookies from the oven and leave to cool on the trays for 2 minutes, before transferring to a wire rack to cool completely. Store in an airtight container for up to four days.

WHOLEMEAL OATCAKES

*These oatcakes are a scrumptious combination of sweet and savoury.
The dough freezes well, so unbaked oatcakes can be frozen for later use –
just cut out and prick the oatcakes (but don't brush with milk), then freeze
between layers of parchment paper. Brush with milk before baking.*

MAKES about 40 biscuits

**300 g (2 cups) whole wheat
 flour**
100 g (1 cup) rolled oats
1 teaspoon baking powder
1 teaspoon salt
150 g (¾ cup) butter, cubed
**100 g (½ cup lightly packed)
 soft brown sugar**
1 egg, lightly beaten
milk, for brushing

*These oatcakes
can be eaten as is,
or topped with a
slice of cheese for
a quick snack.*

1 Preheat a conventional oven to 190°C (375°F/Gas 3). Line two
 baking trays with baking paper.

2 Sift the flour into a large bowl, returning the husks to the bowl.
 Transfer to a food processor, then add the oats, baking powder and
 salt. Pulse briefly to combine. Add the butter and process for about
 10 seconds. Alternatively, the dough can be mixed by hand. Rub the
 butter into the dry ingredients until it resembles fine breadcrumbs.

3 Transfer to a large bowl, stir in the sugar and egg and use your
 hands to combine to make a firm, stiff dough. Halve the dough and
 shape into balls, then knead both halves for about 10 seconds, or
 until just coming together.

4 Roll out half of the dough between sheets of baking paper to about
 5 mm (about ¼ in) thick. Stamp out rounds using a 6 cm or 7 cm
 (2½ in) round pastry cutter. Carefully transfer the rounds to the
 prepared trays. Re-roll any trimmings. Repeat with the remaining
 biscuit dough.

5 Lightly brush the top of each round with milk then prick lightly all
 over with a fork. Bake the oatcakes for 13–15 minutes, or until they
 have turned a slightly darker colour.

6 Remove the oatcakes from the oven and allow to cool on the tray for
 5 minutes before transferring to a wire rack to cool completely.
 Store for up to four days in an airtight container.

CHOCOLATE CHIP COOKIES

These are my absolute favourite cookies. They should be soft and chewy, not hard and crumbly. I often make a large batch and freeze half, so I always have some in the freezer ready to bake when we go camping. Stored in an airtight container they should last up to five days, but they are irresistibly more-ish and for this reason come with a warning!

MAKES about 24 cookies

275 g (2¼ cups) all-purpose flour
1 teaspoon salt
1 teaspoon baking powder
225 g (1 cup) butter, softened
175 g (¾ cup) soft brown sugar
175 g (¾ cup) caster sugar
2 eggs, lightly beaten
200 g (1¼ cups) chocolate chips
100 g (¾ cup) mixed nuts, chopped
1 teaspoon natural vanilla extract

To make these nut-free, just add an extra 100 g (½ cup) of chocolate chips.

1 Sift the flour, salt and baking powder into a large bowl.

2 In a separate bowl, beat together the butter and both sugars with an electric whisk for 4–5 minutes, or until pale and creamy. Gradually beat in the eggs, mixing well after each addition. Don't worry if the mixture starts to curdle.

3 Slowly add the flour mixture and stir until well combined. Stir in the chocolate chips, nuts and vanilla extract. Leave to chill in the refrigerator for 1–2 hours. Although they can be baked immediately, chilling them gives the cookies a better shape and texture.

4 Preheat a conventional oven to 200°C (400°F/Gas 4). Line two baking trays with parchment paper. Take heaped teaspoons of the cookie mixture at a time and quickly roll into balls, then flatten slightly. Place on the trays about 5 cm (2 in) apart. Bake for 10–15 minutes, or until golden, but soft.

5 Remove from the oven and leave the cookies to cool on the trays for 5 minutes, before transferring to a wire rack to cool completely. Pack into an airtight container for transporting to camp.

PEAR AND RASPBERRY LOAF

This delicious loaf makes a wonderful healthy snack. It is perfect for serving to hungry kids and adults returning from camp adventures. You can use frozen mixed berries if fresh are unavailable – there is no need to defrost them before using.

MAKES 1 loaf

180 g (1½ cups) all-purpose flour
a pinch of salt
3½ teaspoons baking soda
80 g (⅓ cup firmly packed) soft brown sugar
1 egg, lightly beaten
125 ml (½ cup) vegetable oil
160 ml (⅔ cup) milk
2 ripe pears, peeled, cored and diced
60 g (½ cup) fresh or frozen raspberries

1 Preheat a conventional oven to 200°C (400°F/Gas 4). Grease and line the base and sides of a 22 x 8 cm (8 x 4 in) loaf (bar) tin or other similar tin with parchment paper.

2 Sift the flour into a bowl with the salt and baking soda. Add the sugar, crumbling any large lumps.

3 In a separate bowl, beat together the egg, oil and milk. Add to the dry ingredients and mix well. Gently fold through the pear and raspberries until just combined. Do not over-mix.

4 Spoon the mixture into the prepared tin and bake for 60 minutes. If the top starts to brown too much, cover with foil for the remaining cooking time. To ensure the loaf is cooked, stick a skewer into the loaf and leave for 5 seconds before removing – if it comes out dry it is cooked.

5 Remove the loaf from the oven and leave to cool in the tin. Wrap in parchment paper and store in an airtight container. Cut into slices to serve.

If making pear and raspberry loaf to serve at home, you need to let the loaf cool before slicing, as it may crumble.

OAT SQUARES

Oat squares are an enduring memory from my childhood in London (we always called them flapjacks). This particular recipe is inspired by the one from my mum's 1961 Marguerite Patten baking book. These delicious squares of oats held together by butter, golden syrup and sugar are simple to make. They are perfect for munching around the campfire, for taking to the beach, or for a delicious treat at the end of a long walk or bike ride. Prepare a batch before you leave home.

MAKES 16 oat squares

175 g (¾ cup) butter or margarine
85 g (⅓ cup) Turbinado (raw) sugar
3 tablespoons golden syrup or honey
a pinch of salt
225 g (2¼ cups) quick-cooking rolled oats

1 Preheat a conventional oven to 200°C (400°F/Gas 4). Grease and line the base and sides of a 21 cm (8 x 8 in) square baking tin, or other similar tin with parchment paper.

2 Melt the butter in a saucepan over medium heat. Add the sugar, golden syrup or honey and salt and stir to combine. Remove from the heat, add the oats and mix well to combine.

3 Press the oat square mixture firmly into the prepared tin, smoothing the top. Bake for 25 minutes if you like chewy oat squares, or for 30 minutes if you prefer them crunchier.

4 Remove from the oven and leave to cool in the tin for 5 minutes, then cut into 16 or 20 pieces. Do not leave for too long or they will harden and be hard to cut. Set the tray aside until completely cool, then re-cut when cool. Remove from the tin and store in an airtight container for up to four days.

CHOCOLATE BROWNIES

You can bake these in a smaller 16 cm (6 in) square tin, but allow 30–35 minutes to cook, as the brownies will be thicker.

These brownies are chewy and delicious – you can choose whether to make them even more decadent by adding chocolate chips, or more 'adult' by adding nuts. I often add hazelnuts, but unsalted macadamias are great too. Sometimes I cut these brownies into tiny squares to make them a one-bite treat. It's easiest to cut them into 16 squares first and then halve each one.

MAKES 16–20 brownies

185 ml (¾ cup) vegetable oil
230 g (1½ cups) soft brown sugar
2 eggs, lightly beaten
1 teaspoon natural vanilla extract
100 g (⅔ cup) chocolate chips or walnuts, hazelnuts or unsalted macadamia nuts, chopped
75 g (½ cup) all-purpose flour
¼ teaspoon baking powder
40 g (⅓ cup) unsweetened cocoa powder

1 Preheat the oven to 200°C (400°F/Gas 4). Grease and line the base and sides of a 21 cm (8 x 8 in) square cake tin. If you don't have this exact size tin, use a similar one, but bear in mind if your tin is larger, the brownies won't be quite as moist.

2 Put the oil and sugar in a large bowl and whisk using electric beaters for about 2 minutes until well combined. Add the eggs and vanilla extract and mix until just blended. Stir in the chocolate chips or nuts and distribute evenly.

3 Sift the flour, baking powder and cocoa into the mixture and fold in, but do not over-mix. Pour into the prepared tin and bake for about 20 minutes. To test if the brownies are cooked, insert a skewer into the middle – it should still be a bit gooey but not have any raw mixture on it.

4 Remove from the oven and allow to cool in the tin for 5 minutes, then carefully lift out using the baking paper and transfer to a wire rack to cool completely. Trim the edges (eating them of course), then cut into 16 or 20 pieces. Brownies can be stored in an airtight container for up to four days, but will start to lose their moistness the longer they are kept.

PREPARE AHEAD MEALS

After arriving at your campsite and spending time setting up your tent, it's always good to know you have a meal ready to go. Preparing something tasty a day or even a week in advance and freezing it means that on your first night of camping you can sit down to a delicious home-cooked meal.

Rather than rushing around trying to throw something together quickly , which often ends up being unhealthy, you can pull out one of these delicious recipes for a satisfying start to your holiday.

Depending on your cooler, these dishes should last you for the first three days of your adventure. With recipes ranging from meatballs in tomato sauce and chilli beef, to teriyaki pork and kofta with yoghurt and pita bread, you should find something that all of the family can enjoy.

SPAGHETTI BOLOGNAISE CHOCK-FULL OF VEGIES

This is probably our family's number one camping recipe. A few days before each trip, I always cook up a large batch. I freeze enough for the first night of our trip, but I often make extra for when we return home again, so once the car has been unpacked and the kids have been scrubbed down we don't have to think about what to cook for dinner that night too!

SERVES 4–6

2 tablespoons vegetable oil or olive oil
600 g (1⅓ lb) good-quality ground beef
1 onion, roughly chopped
3 garlic cloves, crushed
1 large carrot, peeled and grated or finely chopped
1 large zucchini, grated or finely chopped
150 ml (generous ½ cup) red wine (optional)
700 g bottle (24 oz can) tomato purée
2 large field mushrooms or 8–10 button mushrooms, finely chopped (optional)
140 g (1 cup) frozen peas
spaghetti or other pasta, to serve

1 Heat 1 tablespoon of the oil in a large heavy-based saucepan over medium heat. Add the beef, in batches, and fry until brown. Remove and set aside.

2 Heat the remaining oil in the same pan over medium heat. Add the onion and garlic and fry for 5 minutes. Add the carrots and zucchini, and cook for about 5 minutes. Return the meat to the pan and add the wine. Bring to the boil and cook for 1 minute to boil off the alcohol.

3 Add the tomato purée then add about 2 tablespoons water to the empty jar, swirl it around to get any leftover purée and pour into the pan. Add the mushrooms, if using, and season well with salt and freshly ground black pepper. Bring to the boil, then reduce the heat to low, cover, and simmer gently for 1–2 hours – the longer the better.

4 Stir in the peas, then leave to cool completely before transferring to airtight containers and freezing.

AT THE CAMP

5 This dish can be cooked from frozen if necessary. Place in a camp oven or large saucepan and reheat over the fire or a gas cooker. Stir regularly as it cooks, ensuring it reaches boiling point before serving.

Don't forget the spaghetti or pasta! You can also serve this with fresh crusty bread on the side.

Harissa is a spicy condiment made from chillies and spices – it's available from delicatessens and Middle Eastern grocery stores.

KOFTA WITH YOGHURT AND PITA BREAD

I often make these kofta for the adults when I'm making meatballs for the kids. However, kofta can be kid-friendly too, particularly if you leave out the harissa paste, although they aren't that spicy even with harissa. They make a great addition to any gathering and are a cinch to cook on the barbecue.

SERVES 4
(MAKES 10 kofta)

1 teaspoon ground cumin
1 teaspoon ground coriander
2 tablespoons olive oil or vegetable oil, plus extra to serve
1 onion, finely chopped
3 garlic cloves, crushed
2 tablespoons finely chopped fresh coriander (cilantro) leaves
2 tablespoons finely chopped fresh mint leaves
1 teaspoon harissa (optional)
800 g (1¾ lb) good-quality ground lamb or beef
4–8 pita breads, to serve
3 tomatoes, chopped, to serve
green salad leaves, to serve
plain yoghurt, to serve

1 Heat a frying pan over medium–high heat. Add the cumin and coriander and dry-roast for about 1 minute, shaking the pan regularly. Transfer to a large mixing bowl.

2 Heat the oil in the frying pan and fry the onion for 5 minutes over low–medium heat, stirring regularly. Add the garlic and fry for 1 minute. Remove from the heat and transfer to the mixing bowl with the spices.

3 Put the remaining ingredients into the bowl and use your hands to mix well until combined. Divide the mixture into 10 even-sized portions and roll each portion into a fat sausage shape. Put into airtight containers and freeze.

AT THE CAMP

4 Allow the kofta to defrost in your cooler, not in the sun. To cook the kofta, rub or brush them all over with oil to prevent them sticking to the pan. Place on a grill rack over the fire or on a hot barbecue plate and cook for 10–15 minutes, turning regularly, or until just cooked through. Put the pita bread close to the fire to warm through and toast slightly. Open the pita breads and serve the kofta inside, with chopped tomato, salad leaves and yoghurt.

CHILLI BEEF AND VEGETABLES

It's up to you how spicy you make this dish. If you are serving it to kids or adults who don't like chilli, then you can leave the chilli out altogether and make it more of a bean and beef stew. This dish is full of vegetables, so there is no need to serve it with any greens on the side, although you may like to partner it with some rice or crusty bread, a dollop of sour cream and a scattering of grated cheese.

SERVES 4–6

2 tablespoons olive oil
2 onions, finely chopped
2 garlic cloves, crushed
2 carrots, peeled and grated
2 zucchini, finely grated
1 large red capsicum (bell
   pepper), seeded and diced
2–3 small red chillies,
   seeded and finely chopped
1 teaspoon ground cumin
1 teaspoon hot chilli powder
800 g (1¾ lb) good-quality
   ground beef
2 x 400 g (14 oz) cans kidney
   beans, rinsed and drained
2 x 400 g (14 oz) cans cherry
   tomatoes
250 ml (1 cup) tomato purée
1 teaspoon dried oregano
2 tablespoons chopped fresh
   coriander (cilantro)

1. Heat the oil in a large heavy-based saucepan or casserole dish (or in your camp oven if you are making it at the campsite). Add the onion, garlic, carrot, zucchini and bell pepper and fry gently for about 10 minutes.

2. Add the fresh chilli, ground cumin and chilli powder and cook for 1 minute, stirring everything together.

3. Increase the heat to high and add the beef. Cook for 2–3 minutes, stirring until the beef is brown. Add the kidney beans, cherry tomatoes, tomato purée and oregano and season with salt and freshly ground black pepper. Bring to the boil, then reduce the heat to low, cover, and simmer for at least 1 hour. If you prefer your chilli slightly thicker, simmer with the lid off for a further 15 minutes. Stir in the cilantro.

4. Remove from the heat and allow to cool. Transfer to airtight containers and freeze.

AT THE CAMP

5. Allow the chilli beef and vegetables to defrost in the cooler (although it can also be cooked from frozen) then reheat in a saucepan over a fire or gas cooker. Ensure it is piping hot before serving.

YOGHURT AND SPICE-MARINATED CHICKEN

As well as tasting sensational, this yoghurt marinade acts as a tenderiser and helps stop the chicken from drying out as it cooks. If you're making this while camping, don't worry about dry-frying the spices beforehand, just add them straight to the marinade. Leave the meat to develop in the cooler for at least 1 hour before cooking. This marinade also works well with lamb cutlets or pork chops.

SERVES 4

650 g (1½ lb) skinless, boneless free-range chicken thigh or breast fillets, cut into large pieces (if the breast meat is particularly thick, halve horizontally)

YOGHURT SPICE MARINADE
1 teaspoon ground cumin
1 teaspoon ground coriander
200 g (1 cup) plain yoghurt
2 tablespoons apricot chutney

1 To make the marinade, heat a small frying pan over medium heat. Add the cumin and coriander and dry-roast for about 30 seconds, shaking the pan regularly. Tip into a small bowl.

2 Add the yoghurt and chutney to the toasted spices, season with salt and freshly ground black pepper and mix well.

3 Put the chicken into an airtight container and add the yoghurt marinade. Mix everything together well and refrigerate for a few hours to allow the flavours to infuse. Transfer to the freezer and freeze for at least 12 hours.

AT THE CAMP

4 Allow the chicken to defrost in your cooler, not in the sun. If cooking directly over the fire or on a barbecue the chicken will take around 10–15 minutes, turning regularly. Alternatively, you can thread the chicken onto metal skewers, then sit a couple of bricks or rocks on a grill rack over the fire, balancing the skewers between the bricks to prevent them burning. Cooking them this way will take a little longer. Ensure they are cooked through before serving.

TERIYAKI PORK

When I am camping, I often start thinking about what to cook for dinner early in the day. Having a delicious piece of pork loin already marinated means I only need to think about a salad to serve it with. Teriyaki pork is a favourite with my kids, who start milling around the fire as the tantalizing smells begin wafting through the campsite. This marinade will work just as well with chicken or beef.

SERVES 4

80 ml (⅓ cup) soy sauce
80 ml (⅓ cup) mirin
1 teaspoon roasted sesame oil
2 tablespoons honey
1 garlic clove, crushed (optional)
750 g (about 2) pork fillets
green salad and potato salad, to serve

It is important to let the pork rest before serving to ensure it is cooked properly.

1 Combine the soy sauce, mirin and sesame oil in a large shallow dish. Add the honey and stir well. Add the garlic and season with pepper.

2 Cut several shallow slashes across both sides of the pork to allow the marinade to get into the meat. Put the meat into the dish and turn in the marinade a few times to coat. Marinate in the refrigerator for at least 2 hours.

3 Transfer the pork and marinade to a large re-sealable snack bag or airtight container and freeze for at least 12 hours.

AT THE CAMP

4 Allow the pork to defrost in the cooler, not in the sun. Remove the pork from the marinade and if possible, pat dry with paper towel (this helps with getting a nice crisp outside).

5 Cook on a barbecue or grill rack over the fire for 3–4 minutes on each side. At this point, wrap it in foil to prevent the outside burning before the middle is cooked. Move to a cooler part of the barbecue or to the side of the fire and cook for a further 15–20 minutes. The cooking time will depend on the heat, but it is safe to serve the meat when it is still a little pink in the middle.

6 Once cooked, wrap the pork in foil (if not already wrapped) and let it sit for 10 minutes to finish cooking. Slice and serve with the salads.

MEATBALLS IN TOMATO SAUCE

These meatballs have been loved by pretty much every kid and adult who have eaten them. Served with a basic tomato sauce, this recipe is the simplest version that I make, but you can enhance their flavour by adding some freshly chopped parsley or chives, a finely chopped chilli, some chopped black olives, grated courgette (zucchini) or carrot.

SERVES 4
(MAKES 20 meatballs)

80 ml (⅓ cup) milk
2 slices of whole wheat
   bread, crusts removed, cut
   into small pieces
1 tablespoon vegetable oil,
   plus extra
1 onion, finely chopped
1 large garlic clove, crushed
700 g (1½ lb) good-quality
   minced pork or beef
700 g bottle (24 oz can)
   tomato purée
spaghetti or other pasta, to
   serve
grated parmesan or cheddar
   cheese, to serve

1   Put the milk in a small bowl, add the bread and mix to combine. Leave the bread to soak up the milk.

2   Meanwhile, heat the oil in a frying pan over low–medium heat. Add the onion and garlic and cook for 3–4 minutes, or until softened but not browned. Transfer to a mixing bowl and add the mince.

3   Squeeze the milk from the bread and crumble into the mince; discard the milk. Season with salt and freshly cracked black pepper, then use your hands to mix everything together.

4   Take about 1 heaped tablespoon of the mixture at a time and roll into small balls – you should make about 20 meatballs. Arrange in layers in an airtight container, separated by parchment paper, and freeze.

AT THE CAMP

5   Allow the meatballs to defrost in the cooler, not in the sun. Heat a little oil in a large frying pan or camp oven. Fry the meatballs for 5–8 minutes, turning regularly. Pour in the tomato purée, stir gently, then reduce the heat, cover, and simmer for 10 minutes. If the sauce gets too dry, add a little water.

6   Meanwhile, cook the spaghetti according to the packet instructions and serve the meatballs on top with some grated cheese.

GROUND PORK AND VEAL WITH ROOT VEGETABLES

Parsnips add a little sweetness to this dish. If you prefer, ground beef could easily be used instead of pork and veal. My family really enjoys eating this hearty meal, especially when we're camping in the mountains on chilly winter evenings.

SERVES 4–6

2 tablespoons olive oil
600 g (1⅓ lb) good-quality
   mixed ground pork
   and veal
1 large onion, chopped
2 garlic cloves, crushed
2 carrots, peeled and grated
2 parsnips, peeled and grated
1 teaspoon dried oregano or
   parsley
700 g bottle (24 oz can)
   tomato purée
spaghetti or other pasta,
   to serve
grated cheese, to serve

1   Heat 1 tablespoon of the oil in a large casserole dish or heavy-based saucepan over medium heat. Add the pork and veal minces in two batches and cook, stirring occasionally, for 3–4 minutes until browned. Transfer to a bowl.

2   Heat the remaining tablespoon of oil in the same pan over medium heat. Add the onion and garlic and cook gently for about 5 minutes. Add the carrots and parsnips and cook for a further 5 minutes.

3   Return the meat to the pan and stir in the oregano and purée. Add 185 ml (¾ cup) water to the purée bottle or can, swirl it around, then add to the pan, stirring to combine. Season well with salt and freshly ground black pepper.

4   Bring to the boil, then reduce the heat to low, cover, and simmer for 1 hour. Remove from the heat and cool completely before transferring to airtight containers and freezing.

AT THE CAMP

5   This dish can be cooked from frozen. Place in a camp oven or heavy-based saucepan and sit it to one side of the fire or over a low gas cooker and stir regularly. Ensure it reaches boiling point before serving. Serve with cooked spaghetti and grated cheese.

CAJUN FISH FILLETS

Serve with salad and don't forget a lemon for squeezing over the fish.

Pretty much any white fish fillet can be used for this dish, although it's best to avoid very thin fillets as they don't defrost very well. You can also make this at the campsite if you have a fisher-person in your party – just don't forget to bring the store cupboard ingredients with you.

SERVES 4

1 tablespoon Cajun spice mix
2 teaspoons ground paprika
1 tablespoon lemon juice
2 tablespoons olive oil
2 garlic cloves, crushed
1 teaspoon freshly ground
    black pepper
700–800 g (1½ to 2 lb) firm
    white fish fillets, such as
    cod, tilapia or rockfish
lemon wedges, to serve
green salad, to serve

1 In a bowl, combine the Cajun spice mix, paprika, lemon juice, olive oil, garlic and black pepper. Rub all over the fish fillets, gently massaging the marinade into the flesh.

2 Place in the refrigerator for a couple of hours to allow the flavours to penetrate into the fish. Transfer to a re-sealable snack bag or airtight container and freeze for at least 24 hours.

AT THE CAMP

3 Allow the fish to defrost in the cooler, not in the sun. Cook on a barbecue hot plate or over a fire for about 4 minutes on each side. This is the timing for fish that is about 2 cm (¾ in) thick; if your fish is any thicker it will take longer. Do not overcook the fish or it will become dry. Serve with lemon wedges and a simple green salad on the side.

MARINATED FISH FILLETS

This tasty marinade relies on fresh coriander (cilantro) and a mixture of tasty spices for its unique flavour – you can make it in advance or at the campsite. If you've got a fire going, wrap some potatoes in foil and bake for 45–60 minutes in the hot coals to serve alongside the fish for a memorable fireside dinner.

SERVES 4

1 teaspoon ground coriander
1 teaspoon ground cumin
1 teaspoon ground ginger
2 tablespoons olive oil
2 garlic cloves, crushed
1 teaspoon harissa paste
2 tablespoons chopped fresh
   coriander (cilantro) leaves
4 x 180–200 g (⅓–½ lb)
   salmon, cod, snapper or
   other firm fish fillets

When you are choosing fish, buy thicker fillets as they freeze and defrost better than thin ones.

1 Heat a small frying pan over medium heat. Add the ground coriander, cumin and ginger and dry-roast for about 1 minute, shaking the pan regularly. Transfer to a small bowl.

2 Add the oil, garlic, harissa and coriander leaves to the bowl with the spices, season with salt and freshly ground black pepper, and mix well.

3 Place the fish fillets into a re-sealable snack bag and add the marinade. Massage the fish gently to coat. Place in the refrigerator for a couple of hours to allow the flavours to penetrate. Freeze for at least 24 hours.

AT THE CAMP

4 Defrost the fish in your cooler, not in the sun. Cook the fish on a barbecue or on a grill rack over the fire for about 5 minutes on each side, or cook in a pan on a gas cooker. Cooking times will depend on the thickness of your fish. If the fire is very hot, sit the fish at the edge, otherwise the outside will burn before the inside is cooked. Do not overcook the fish, or it will be dry.

VEGETABLE AND CHICKPEA CASSEROLE

This dish is reminiscent of a French-style ratatouille, but with extra vegetables and chickpeas. It can be served as a main meal with couscous or as an accompaniment to grilled meat and fish. Alternatively, for a quick meal, serve cold with slices of crusty bread.

**SERVES 4
(or 8 as an accompaniment)**

60 ml (¼ cup) olive oil
1 large onion, halved and
   thinly sliced
1 red capsicum (bell pepper),
   seeded and cut into thin
   strips
2 garlic cloves, crushed
2 eggplants, halved
   lengthwise and cut into
   1 cm (⅓ in) slices
2 zucchini, cut into 1 cm
   (⅓ in) slices
400 g (14 oz) can diced
   tomatoes
400 g (14 oz) can chickpeas,
   rinsed and drained
½ teaspoon ground coriander
1 small handful fresh basil
   leaves, roughly torn
grated parmesan cheese,
   to serve

1 Heat 2 tablespoons of the oil in a large heavy-based casserole dish or saucepan over medium heat. Add the onion and cook for about 5 minutes, or until soft.

2 Add the bell pepper, garlic, eggplant, zucchini and remaining oil. Stir well, cover, and cook over low heat for 25–30 minutes, stirring occasionally. The heat needs to be not so low that nothing happens, but not too hot that it dries out.

3 Add the tomatoes, chickpeas and coriander. Season with salt and freshly ground black pepper, cover again, and simmer for a further 20 minutes, or until the vegetables are soft but not mushy.

4 Stir in the basil and leave to cool completely. Transfer to an airtight container and freeze for at least 12 hours.

AT THE CAMP

5 This dish can be cooked from frozen or partially frozen. Place in a camp oven or heavy-based saucepan and sit to one side of the fire so it doesn't get too hot. As it heats you need to stir it regularly. Alternatively, you can cook it in a saucepan over a gas cooker. Ensure it reaches boiling point before serving. Serve with parmesan cheese scattered over the top, if desired.

CATCH OF THE DAY

The biggest problem with taking fish to the campsite with you is that it won't keep for any longer than a day in the cooler. The recipes in this chapter are most suitable for the first day of your trip when you have brought some fresh fish with you, or for those lucky enough to catch it fresh.

The type of fish you use may vary depending on whether you catch it yourself, but I have specified a couple of varieties to suit each dish. So, if the fisher-people among you catch something fresh, you might like to try the foil-wrapped fillets with tomatoes, olives and herbs or the quick fish kebabs. If you can get to a fishmonger, the easy fish stew would make a perfect fireside meal.

FOIL WRAPPED FILLETS OF FISH WITH TOMATOES, OLIVES AND HERBS

The best way to transport and store fresh herbs for a camping trip is to prepare and pack them before you leave home. Rinse them under cold water, then shake off any excess and wrap in damp paper towel. Place in a small airtight container and store in the refrigerator until you set off, then store in your cooler until needed.

SERVES 4

olive oil
4 skinless, boneless white or
    pink fish fillets
250 g (9 oz) cherry tomatoes,
    halved
about 20 pitted black olives
1 small handful fresh herbs,
    such as cilantro or flat-leaf
    parsley, chopped

Don't forget the foil.

1 Tear off 8 pieces of foil, large enough to enclose a piece of fish and some vegetables. Make 4 double layers of foil – these will create individual parcels for cooking.

2 Drizzle a little bit of olive oil onto the top pieces of foil and smear it around. Place a fish fillet into the centre of each one. Divide the cherry tomatoes and olives between the fish and scatter over the herbs. Drizzle with a little more olive oil and season with salt and freshly ground black pepper. Carefully enclose the fish.

3 Place the fish parcels on a grill rack over the fire or on a barbecue and cook for about 18–20 minutes, or until the fish is cooked. Unwrap the fish carefully and simply sit the foil parcels in bowls so you won't lose the delicious juices when unwrapping them.

4 Serve the fish in the foil accompanied by rice, potatoes or pasta.

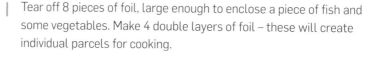

QUICK FISH KEBABS

Although you could use wooden skewers for these kebabs, if you are cooking over a fire you may find they burn too quickly, so metal ones are better. If you do use wooden ones, soak them in water for 20 minutes beforehand to prevent them from burning during cooking.

**SERVES 4
(MAKES 8 kebabs)**

800 g (1¾ lb) skinless,
  boneless firm fish fillets,
  such as cod, salmon or
  haddock
2 small courgettes (zucchini),
  cut into 16 slices
1 small red or yellow
  capsicum (bell pepper),
  seeded and cut into
  16 pieces
juice of ½ lemon
2 tablespoons olive oil, plus
  extra for brushing

Don't forget the skewers.

1 Cut the fish into 3 cm (1¼ in) cubes and put into a large bowl with the zucchini and pepper. In a separate bowl, combine the lemon juice and olive oil and season with salt and freshly ground black pepper. Pour over the fish and vegetables and toss to coat.

2 Divide the fish and vegetables evenly between the skewers, alternating between ingredients.

3 Grease a grill rack with oil then sit the kebabs over the fire or on a barbecue. Make sure you do not cook them too close to the fire, as you need the vegetables to cook without burning the fish.

4 Cook for about 12–15 minutes, turning regularly and brushing with any remaining oil and lemon juice. Ensure all sides of the fish get cooked as they can twist while being turned. Serve the kebabs with salad and potatoes, or pasta.

PESTO FISH WITH BEAN SALAD

It doesn't really matter what fish you use for this recipe, but it is preferable if it is skinless and boneless. If you've caught something fresh, just clean and fillet the fish and try and give it some time to soak in the marinade. If you absolutely can't wait, it will still taste great.

SERVES 4

4 x 180–200 g (⅓–½ lb)
   skinless, boneless
   fish fillets
4 tablespoons pesto
olive oil or vegetable oil, for
   brushing

BEAN SALAD
60 ml (¼ cup) olive oil
2 tablespoons lemon juice
400 g (14 oz) can kidney or
   cannellini beans, rinsed
   and drained
250 g (9 oz) cherry tomatoes,
   halved or quartered
1 small cucumber, chopped
2 handfuls rocket (arugula) or
   mixed salad leaves

1 Put the fish onto a plate and rub the pesto all over both sides of each fillet. Set aside in the cooler for 1 hour to marinate.

2 Meanwhile, make the bean salad. Whisk together the olive oil and lemon juice and season with salt and freshly ground black pepper. Combine the remaining salad ingredients in a serving bowl, pour over the dressing and toss well.

3 Place the fish on a lightly oiled grill rack over the fire or on a barbecue and cook for 2 minutes. Brush the tops with oil, then carefully turn over and cook for a further 2 minutes, or until the fish is just cooked – the cooking time will depend on this thickness of your fish.

4 Serve the pesto fish with the bean salad.

Don't forget the pesto.

QUICK MILD FISH CURRY

Use white fish fillets for this recipe. You can either make this as a Thai-style curry or an Indian curry, depending on which curry paste you choose — Thai green, Massaman or a mild Indian curry paste all work really well. Vary the amount of curry paste to suit your family's spice tolerance.

SERVES 4

1 tablespoon vegetable or olive oil
1 onion, roughly chopped
2 garlic cloves, roughly chopped
1–2 tablespoons curry paste
600 g (1⅓ lb) white fish fillets, such as haddock or cod, cut into bite-sized pieces
2 x 400 g (14 oz) cans coconut milk
125 g (1 cup) baby corn, quartered
200 g (1 cup) snow peas, sliced
1 handful coriander (cilantro) leaves (optional), to serve
steamed rice, to serve

1 Heat the oil in a camp oven or heavy-based saucepan. Add the onion and garlic, cover, and cook over low heat for 5–10 minutes, stirring regularly until the onions are golden brown and developing a good flavour.

2 Stir in the curry paste and cook for 1 minute. Add the fish, stir to coat in the paste mixture, then add the coconut milk. Cover and bring to the boil, then place over a gentler heat and simmer for 5 minutes.

3 Add the baby corn and snow peas and cook for about 3 minutes. Scatter over the cilantro leaves, if using, and serve the hot curry with steamed rice.

Don't forget to take some fresh cilantro with you. If you have any leftover coriander, you can use it in a salad or in a marinade.

EASY FISH AND VEGETABLE STEW

You can use almost any fresh fish for this stew, although avoid using oily fish such as mackerel. The sugar is used to counterbalance the acidity of the wine and tomatoes, but isn't vital. You can also add carrots to this stew if you have some. Roughly chop and add them at the same time as the potatoes.

SERVES 4

2 tablespoons olive oil
1 onion, halved and thinly
　　sliced
2 garlic cloves, crushed
12 small waxy potatoes,
　　quartered
250 ml (1 cup) white wine
400 g (14 oz) can chopped
　　tomatoes
600 g (1⅓ lb) skinless,
　　boneless fish fillets, cut
　　into bite-sized pieces
1 handful green beans,
　　trimmed and cut into
　　3 cm (1¼ in) lengths
2 teaspoons sugar (optional)

1　Heat the oil in a camp oven or large heavy-based frying pan over a fire or gas cooker. Add the onion and garlic, cover, and cook for 5–10 minutes, stirring regularly until light golden.

2　Add the potato and cook for a couple of minutes. Pour in the wine and let it boil for a minute or two, scraping the base of the pan with a wooden spoon.

3　Add the tomatoes and about 125 ml (½ cup) water, or just enough to ensure the potatoes are submerged. Cover with a lid and simmer for about 25 minutes, or until the potatoes are tender when pierced with a fork.

4　Add the fish, beans and sugar, if using, and season well with salt and freshly ground black pepper. Cover and cook for 5 minutes, or until the beans are tender and the fish is cooked.

5　Divide the fish stew between bowls and serve immediately.

FISH FILLETS WITH CRUNCHY ASIAN COLESLAW

Most kids like sweet chilli sauce, so don't worry about the coleslaw being too spicy. This recipe is really all about the salad. If making this in advance, don't add the dressing until you are ready to serve, otherwise the cabbage will wilt.

SERVES 4–6

4–6 fish fillets, such as snapper or salmon
olive oil, for brushing

ASIAN COLESLAW
¼ Chinese cabbage or white cabbage
¼ red cabbage
1 carrot, grated
about 30 snow peas, thinly sliced
juice of 1 lime
2 tablespoons fish sauce
2 tablespoons sweet chilli sauce

1 To make the Asian coleslaw, remove the core from both cabbages, then shred each cabbage into short strips widthwise. Place in a large bowl with the carrot and snow peas and toss to combine.

2 In a small separate bowl, combine the lime juice, fish sauce and sweet chilli sauce. Pour over the coleslaw and toss to combine. Set aside while cooking the fish.

3 Brush the fish all over with olive oil and season with salt and freshly ground black pepper. Cook the fish on a grill rack over the fire or on a barbecue for about 4 minutes on each side, or until just cooked through – the exact cooking time will depend on the thickness of the fish.

4 To serve, divide the coleslaw between serving plates and place a fillet of fish on top.

Don't forget the sweet chilli and fish sauces.

FIRE UP THE BARBECUE

There is nothing quite like eating a meal that has been cooked on a barbecue, especially when you are eating it under the stars in the great outdoors. This chapter is full of recipes that lend themselves to this kind of experience. Many campsites provide wood-fired barbecues and lots of campers take their own portable barbecues with them. I highly recommend investing in a grill rack with legs (available from most camping stores) so you can build your own fire and sit this over the top – it's hard to beat the flavour of meat that has been cooked over an open flame. You can create a makeshift grill by sitting a metal tray or rack over a fire, held up by bricks or logs.

Many of the recipes in this chapter can be marinated and frozen at home – they will defrost slowly in your cooler and can be pulled out for a relaxed and delectable barbecue meal.

SWEET CHILLI CHICKEN BAGUETTES

These baguettes are popular with my whole family and work just as well served for lunch or dinner. They are also great for taking on a picnic lunch – wrap the just-cooked baguettes in foil or baking paper for easy transport and eat them when you get to your destination. It is best to eat them within 30 minutes of cooking the chicken, if possible. If the kids prefer softer bread rolls, serve these instead of baguettes.

SERVES 4–6

4 x 200 g (½ lb) chicken breasts, preferably free-range
80 ml (⅓ cup) sweet chilli sauce
1 baguette, cut into 10 cm (4 in) lengths or 4–6 soft bread rolls
good-quality egg mayonnaise
lettuce or rocket (arugula) leaves
1 avocado, pit removed, flesh thinly sliced

1 Try and get chicken breasts of equal thickness to make cooking them easier. Slice the thinner end off each breast, then cut the thicker end in half horizontally through the middle to make thinner fillets of chicken. Place the chicken in a bowl, add the sweet chilli sauce and turn to coat the chicken. Return to your cooler for 1 hour to marinate if you have the time, but it's not essential.

2 Cook the chicken on a barbecue over medium heat, or on a grill rack over the fire. If cooking over the fire, cook to one side, otherwise the outside will burn before the middle is cooked. Cook for 4–6 minutes on each side, or until cooked through – the time will depend on the heat and the thickness of the chicken.

3 Meanwhile, split the baguettes and spread both sides with mayonnaise. Top with lettuce and avocado. When the chicken is cooked, add slices to each baguette and serve.

SWEET AND SPICY CHICKEN PIECES

Adding chilli to this dish is optional, depending on how hot you like your food. Although marinating the chicken for hours isn't vital, if you get the chance to leave it in the cooler for a few hours while you're at the beach or on a hike it will improve the flavour. Serve with baked potatoes and salad, or wrap in pita pockets with some yoghurt and salad for an easy meal.

SERVES 4–6

2 tablespoons olive oil
2 tablespoons honey
2 tablespoons soy sauce
1 garlic clove, crushed
2 teaspoons mustard or
   1 teaspoon mustard powder
½ teaspoon chilli powder
1 kg (2⅓ lb) chicken pieces,
   bone in (or 800 g/1¾ lb
   boneless pieces),
   preferably free-range
green salad and baked
   potatoes, to serve

Don't forget the honey and spices.

1 Combine the olive oil, honey, soy sauce, garlic, mustard and chilli powder in a small bowl. Add some freshly ground black pepper, but not salt as the soy sauce is already salty.

2 Cut a few slashes into each piece of chicken and place in a dish. Pour over the marinade and massage into the chicken for a couple of minutes. If making this in advance, cover and place in the cooler, making sure it is sitting flat, so the marinade doesn't leak.

3 If using bone-in chicken, cook on a barbecue for about 25 minutes, turning often and brushing regularly with the marinade until cooked through. Do not brush with the marinade for the final 5 minutes of cooking, to ensure the marinade is cooked. Boneless chicken pieces will take about 15 minutes to cook, depending on their thickness.

4 Transfer the chicken to a clean plate and serve with a green salad and baked potatoes on the side.

MARINATED BUTTERFLIED LEG OF LAMB

If you don't want to take multiple jars of spices to the campsite with you, simply combine the coriander, cumin and mint in one small jar before you leave home and add to the remaining ingredients before cooking. If you have any leftovers, a lamb and chutney sandwich will win hearts the next day!

SERVES about 8

2–2.5 kg (4½ to 5½ lb) leg of lamb, boned and butterflied (a little less without bone)
80 ml (⅓ cup) olive oil
juice of 1 lemon
1 teaspoon ground coriander
1 teaspoon ground cumin
2 teaspoons dried mint leaves
2 garlic cloves, crushed
green salad and baked potatoes, to serve

Get your butcher to butterfly the leg of lamb and vacuum pack it. This should help keep it fresh for a few extra days.

1 Open the lamb out and use a sharp knife to make a few slashes through the thickest part of the meat – this helps the meat cook evenly.

2 In a bowl, combine the olive oil, lemon juice, coriander, cumin, mint leaves and garlic. Rub the marinade all over the lamb. If possible, return the meat to the cooler (place it on a tray or even in a clean plastic bag) and leave to marinate for 1–2 hours. Ideally you would prepare this in the morning and allow it to marinate all day.

3 When you're ready to cook, ensure your barbecue or fire isn't too hot, otherwise your meat will char on the outside and still be raw in the middle. Cook the meat on a barbecue for 15 minutes, then turn over and cook for a further 15 minutes. If you are cooking on a hooded barbecue put the hood down for the second 15 minutes. If not, try and cover your meat with foil. If you can't do either, don't worry.

4 Check to see if the meat is cooked to your liking, remembering it will cook further while it rests. If it's ready, remove from the heat, wrap in foil and leave to rest for about 10 minutes. Slice into thick slices and serve with salad and baked potatoes.

VIETNAMESE PORK MEATBALLS WITH NOODLES

These meatballs are quick and easy to make and can be served on their own, without the noodles or dressing. Sometimes I make big ones, but at other times, particularly if I'm feeding a crowd, I make them half the size.

SERVES 4–6

MEATBALLS
800 g (1¾ lb) good-quality
   minced pork
1 small red chilli, seeded and
   finely chopped (optional)
3 garlic cloves, crushed
1½ tablespoons fish sauce
3 tablespoons finely chopped
   mint leaves
3 tablespoons finely chopped
   coriander (cilantro) leaves
250 g (9 oz) packet rice
   vermicelli noodles, to serve

VIETNAMESE DRESSING
2 tablespoons fish sauce
½ small red chilli, seeded
   and finely chopped
1½ tablespoons lime juice
1 teaspoon sugar

1 Put all of the meatball ingredients into a bowl, season well with salt and freshly ground black pepper and use your hands to mix well until the pork turns a paler pink. Taking a tablespoon of the mixture at a time, roll into neat balls – you should make about 16 in total. Alternatively, take 2 teaspoons at a time to make 32 smaller balls. These can be made in advance and chilled in the cooler.

2 To make the Vietnamese dressing, put all of the ingredients into a small bowl and stir to dissolve the sugar. Set aside.

3 Cook the meatballs on a medium–hot barbecue or on a grill rack over the fire for 10–12 minutes for the larger ones, or 8–9 minutes for the smaller meatballs, turning regularly, until just cooked through. Be careful not to overcook, otherwise they will become dry.

4 Meanwhile, cook the noodles in boiling water for 2 minutes, or according to the packet instructions. Drain and rinse in cold water to cool. To serve, pour the dressing over the noodles and toss to combine, then sit the meatballs on top. Alternatively, serve the meatballs, noodles and dressing separately, allowing each person to help themselves.

Don't forget the vermicelli and fish sauce.

PESTO LAMB BURGERS

*Nearly everyone loves a good burger and homemade or camp-made are best.
These are so simple the kids can get involved too. This recipe makes four large burgers,
but you could easily make eight smaller ones, if preferred. The pesto flavour
is quite mild, so add the extra tablespoon if you really love it.*

MAKES 4 large burgers

PESTO LAMB PATTIES
800 g (1¾ lb) good-quality
   ground lamb
2 garlic cloves, crushed
2–3 tablespoons pesto

4–8 burger buns or soft rolls,
   to serve
crisp lettuce leaves, to serve
sliced tomato, to serve
sliced cucumber, to serve
balsamic onion relish (page
   154), to serve

1 Put the lamb, garlic and pesto into a large bowl and season with salt and freshly ground black pepper. Use your hands to combine well.

2 Divide the lamb mixture into 4 or 8 portions, depending on whether you would like to make large or small burgers, then shape into patties. The burgers can be prepared ahead and stored in the cooler, if desired.

3 Cook the patties on a barbecue or on a grill rack over the fire for about 6 minutes on each side for larger burgers, or 4–5 minutes on each side for smaller burgers.

4 To assemble the burgers, split the burger buns or rolls and toast them, cut-side down, for 1–2 minutes to warm through.

5 Serve each burger inside a bun with as much lettuce, tomato and cucumber as desired, then top with the balsamic onion relish.

*Don't forget
the pesto.*

SPANISH TORTILLA

This recipe is useful for using up any leftover potatoes from the previous night's dinner. If you don't have any, you'll need to cook some before you start preparing the tortilla. I often serve this for breakfast before heading out on a long walk to keep hunger at bay for as long as possible.

For added bite add a chopped red chilli, some chilli flakes or a few dashes of Tabasco sauce.

SERVES 4–6

2 tablespoons olive oil
4 bacon slices, rind removed, roughly chopped
1 small onion, thinly sliced
225 g (1½ cups) cooked potatoes, roughly chopped or sliced
1 garlic clove, crushed (optional)
8 eggs
80 ml (⅓ cup) milk
60 g (⅔ cups) grated cheddar or tasty cheese
toast, to serve

1 Put the oil in a frying pan with a 26–28 cm (10–11 in) diameter base. Sit on a barbecue or over the fire. Add the bacon and onion and cook for 5 minutes, stirring regularly. Add the potato and garlic, if using, and cook for a further 5 minutes to heat through.

2 Meanwhile, crack the eggs into a bowl or jug and beat to combine. Add the milk, season with salt and freshly cracked black pepper, and mix briefly. Pour into the pan, shaking to cover the vegetables evenly.

3 Scatter the cheese over the top and cook for 2 minutes. Using a spatula or fork, gently pull the cooked egg from the edge of the pan into the centre, tilting the pan so the uncooked egg flows to the base and sides.

4 Cook for a further 1 minute, then cover with a lid or foil and cook for a further 8 minutes, or until the egg is just set.

5 Remove from the heat and let the tortilla sit for 1–2 minutes before turning out onto a board and slicing into wedges. Alternatively, serve straight from the pan in wedges, accompanied by warm toast.

CAMP-MADE SAUSAGES

Although it's easy to buy sausages, knowing you've made your own is very satisfying and comes with the added bonus of knowing exactly what's gone into them! You can vary the flavour by adding 2 tablespoons chopped fresh parsley, a scant ½ teaspoon chilli powder or 3 teaspoons fennel seeds.

MAKES 8 sausages

2 slices of bread, crusts removed
60 ml (¼ cup) milk
800 g (1¾ lb) good-quality ground pork or beef
2 garlic cloves, crushed
1 onion, finely chopped
2 teaspoons chopped fresh thyme or 1 teaspoon dried
olive or vegetable oil, for cooking
8 crusty bread rolls or slices bread, to serve
salad leaves, such as rocket (arugula) or lettuce, to serve
mustard or tomato sauce, to serve

1 To make the sausages, break the bread into small pieces and put in a small bowl. Pour over the milk and leave to soak for 5 minutes.

2 Put the milk-soaked bread in a bowl with the mince, garlic, onion and thyme (and any extra flavourings if you're using them). Season with salt and plenty of freshly ground black pepper and use your hands to mix thoroughly for 3–4 minutes, or until well combined.

3 Divide the mixture into 8 even-sized portions and shape each into a fat sausage shape (you may find this easier with slightly wet hands). If you have the time, place on a plate or wrap in plastic wrap and put in the cooler for 30 minutes, or up to 4 hours. Chilling them slightly helps them hold their shape when cooking, although it's not essential.

4 Brush or rub the sausages all over with a little oil and cook on a barbecue or on a grill rack over the fire for 15–20 minutes, turning regularly and brushing with oil until they are cooked through.

5 Serve the sausages in bread rolls, accompanied by salad leaves and mustard or sauce.

MARINATED PORK LOIN WITH GREEK SALAD

Pork loin (fillet) is a fairly quick-cooking meat, but be careful that you don't burn the outside before the inside is sufficiently cooked. It is important to rest the meat afterwards so it can finish cooking.

SERVES 4–6

60 ml (¼ cup) olive oil
2 tablespoons lemon juice
2 teaspoons dried oregano
800 g (1¾ lb) pork fillet
   (about 2)
pita bread, to serve (optional)

GREEK SALAD
½ small red onion, thinly
   sliced
3 firm, ripe tomatoes,
   roughly chopped
2 small cucumbers, cubed
1 handful black olives
200 g (7 oz) feta cheese,
   crumbled
olive oil, for drizzling

1 Combine the olive oil, lemon juice and oregano in a shallow dish and season with salt and freshly ground black pepper.

2 Cut several shallow slashes across both sides of the pork to allow the marinade to get into the meat. Put the meat into the dish and turn in the marinade a few times to coat. Set aside in the cooler for at least 2 hours to marinate.

3 Remove the pork from the marinade and if possible, pat dry with paper towel – this helps to get the outside nice and crisp.

4 Cook the pork on a barbecue or grill rack over the fire for 3–4 minutes on each side. Wrap the meat in foil to prevent the outside burning before the middle is cooked. Move to a cooler part of the barbecue or to the side of the fire and continue cooking for about 15 minutes – it is safe to serve the meat when it is still a little pink in the middle.

5 Once cooked, let the foil-wrapped pork rest for 10 minutes – this is important for it to finish cooking. If you didn't wrap it during cooking then cover the pork with a bowl while resting.

6 If serving with pita bread, place over the heat briefly, turning once, until lightly toasted and warmed through.

7 While the pork is resting, make the Greek salad. Combine the onion, tomato, cucumber and olives in a serving bowl. Crumble the feta cheese on top and drizzle with olive oil. Slice the pork and serve with Greek salad and pita bread, if desired.

PORK KEBABS WITH FLAVOURED MAYONNAISE

*It's up to you how you flavour the mayonnaise, you can add your favourite
fresh herbs, a little chilli, a squeeze of lemon juice, a dollop of mustard,
or experiment with a combination to find the right mix for you!*

SERVES 4 (MAKES 8 kebabs)

2 tablespoons hoisin sauce
2 tablespoons soy sauce
450–500 g (1 lb) pork fillet,
    cut into about 24 cubes
16 small brown mushrooms
2 small zucchini, cut into
    1 cm (⅓ in) slices
1 red capsicum (bell pepper),
    seeded and cut into 3 cm
    (1¼ in) squares
olive or vegetable oil, for
    brushing
salad and pita bread, to serve
    (optional)

**MUSTARD AND HERB
MAYONNAISE**
120 g (½ cup) good-quality
    mayonnaise
1 tablespoon lemon juice
1 tablespoon finely chopped
    fresh herbs, such as
    parsley, coriander
    (cilantro), tarragon or
    dill (optional)
1 tablespoon Dijon or
    wholegrain mustard
1 small red chilli, seeded
    (optional)

1 If using wooden skewers, soak 8 of them in water for 20 minutes
   to prevent them from burning during cooking.

2 Combine the hoisin and soy sauces in a medium-sized bowl and
   season with freshly ground black pepper. Add the pork and toss to
   coat. Cover and leave to marinate in the cooler for at least 1 hour
   if you have time; if not they will still taste delicious.

3 Meanwhile, make the mustard and herb mayonnaise. Combine the
   mayonnaise with your choice of ingredients in a small bowl. Stir in
   1 teaspoon water and set aside. If you're not adding lemon juice, add
   a couple more teaspoons of water.

4 Thread the pork onto the skewers alternately with the vegetables.
   Pour any remaining marinade over the vegetables. Brush or drizzle
   each kebab with oil.

5 Preheat a barbecue grill plate to medium and cook the kebabs for
   about 10 minutes, turning regularly, or until the pork is cooked.

6 Serve the kebabs with the mustard and herb mayonnaise and salad.
   If serving as a wrap, cover the pita bread in foil and warm on the
   barbecue for about 5 minutes before serving. Pull the pork
   and vegetables from the skewers and add a dollop
   of the mayonnaise.

*Don't forget the
hoisin and soy sauces
and your choice of
flavourings for the
mayonnaise.*

ONE-POT DINNERS

Going camping often involves sitting around and enjoying your own company while the kids rush around playing games and exploring. The meals in this chapter are perfect for preparing late in the afternoon, when you have time to relax and enjoy the peace and quiet. I like to chop the onion and garlic, throw them into the pot and get the cooking started early, then add the main ingredients and leave it to simmer away on the fire for several hours, checking its progress every now and then. When the hungry hordes descend for dinner you will have a dish equal to any meal cooked in a domestic kitchen.

For most recipes in this chapter you will need a decent heavy-based saucepan, casserole dish or camp oven, but once you've got that, there are endless 'one-pot' meals you can create – our family favours the massaman lamb curry and the ever-popular beef, mushroom and red wine casserole. You'll also find plenty of takers for the pot-roasted pork with potato and pears and any of the tasty vegetable or chicken casseroles. The beauty of most of these dishes is that you don't need to serve them with anything else – once they're cooked, the meal is good to eat straight from the pot!

CHICKEN AND ROOT VEGETABLE STEW

Don't rush the step of cooking the onions, as they will help give this dish its depth of flavour. Adding the fennel is optional, but does give a delicious aniseed flavour to the stew, so buy some before your trip if you can.

SERVES 4

- 2 tablespoons olive oil or vegetable oil
- 1 onion, chopped
- 2 garlic cloves, crushed
- 2 carrots, sliced
- 300 g (1½ cups) winter squash, diced
- 1 large fennel bulb, sliced (optional)
- 800 g (1¾ lb) skinless, boneless chicken thigh or breast fillets, cut into large pieces
- 200 ml (¾ cup or a small wine glass) white wine
- 12 waxy potatoes, quartered

1   Heat the oil in a large camp oven or casserole dish on a grill rack over the fire. Add the onion and garlic and cook for 10 minutes, stirring regularly until they start to turn golden and caramelise – ensure the pot isn't too hot, or they will burn.

2   Add the carrot, squash and fennel and cook for about 5 minutes, stirring every now and then. Add the chicken, stir well to combine and cook for 2–3 minutes, or until the chicken is starting to brown. Add the wine and bring to the boil for about 1 minute to cook off the alcohol.

3   Add 420 ml (1⅔ cups) water, then add the potato and season well with salt and freshly ground black pepper. Cover and bring to the boil, then move to the side of the fire or over the coals away from the direct heat and cook for a further 30–40 minutes, or until the chicken is cooked through and the potato is very tender. Check the seasoning and adjust as desired, then serve in bowls.

BEEF, MUSHROOM, POTATO AND RED WINE CASSEROLE

You can make life at the campsite a bit easier by putting the flour and cumin in a large re-sealable snack bag before you leave home. Then, when you come to cook dinner at the campsite, you just need to put the cubes of meat into the bag and shake it in the pre-seasoned flour. This recipe can easily be doubled to serve more if you're camping with several families, just make sure you have a big enough pot to cook it in!

SERVES 4–6

60 ml (¼ cup) olive oil
  or vegetable oil
2 onions, chopped
3 garlic cloves, crushed
2–3 carrots, peeled
  and sliced
2 tablespoons all-purpose
  flour
½ teaspoon ground cumin
800 g–1 kg (1¾–2¼ lb) cubed
  beef blade steak
250 ml (1 cup) red wine
400 g (14 oz) can
  diced tomatoes
3–4 large potatoes,
  roughly chopped
3–4 field mushrooms,
  roughly chopped

1   Heat the oil in a large camp oven or casserole dish on a grill rack over the fire. Add the onion and garlic and cook for 10 minutes, stirring regularly, until softened. Add the carrots and cook for a further 5 minutes.

2   Meanwhile, put the flour and cumin in a re-sealable snack bag or clean plastic bag and season with salt and freshly ground black pepper. Add the meat and shake it well to coat the beef cubes. Add to the dish, making sure it is on the hottest part of the fire, stirring for a few minutes until the meat is light brown on all sides.

3   Add the wine to the dish and bring to the boil, stir using a wooden spoon to scrape any bits stuck to the base of the dish. Cook for 1 minute, then add the tomatoes and ½ a can of water (use the tomato can) and move to a cooler part of the fire away from direct heat. Cover and simmer gently for about 40 minutes.

4   Add the potatoes and mushrooms to the dish and cook for 30–35 minutes. Stir everything around and let the potatoes break down in the sauce.

5   Remove from the fire and set aside for 5 minutes. Adjust the seasoning as desired, then divide the casserole between bowls and serve.

MASSAMAN LAMB CURRY WITH POTATOES

This is a delicious and warming Thai curry that will cope with sitting over an open fire for several hours. If cooking over gas, once the coconut milk and tomatoes are in, cook for about 40 minutes, then add the potatoes and cook for a further 20 minutes, or until the potatoes are cooked.

SERVES 4–6

2 tablespoons vegetable oil
1 onion, sliced
2 garlic cloves, crushed
4 tablespoons Massaman
   curry paste
2 carrots, chopped
400 g (2 cups) butternut
   squash, cubed
1 kg (2¼ lb) cubed boneless
   lamb leg
2 x 400 ml (14 oz) cans
   coconut milk
400 g (14 oz) can tomatoes
10 waxy potatoes, quartered
   or chopped if large

Waxy potatoes hold their shape better than floury ones, so they won't disintegrate into the curry.

1 Heat the vegetable oil in a large camp oven or in a casserole dish on a grill rack over the fire. Add the onion and garlic and cook for 8–10 minutes, stirring regularly. Add the curry paste, stir well and cook for a couple of minutes until fragrant smells waft from the pan.

2 Add the carrot, squash and lamb, stirring to coat in the paste. Cook for 5 minutes, then add the coconut milk and tomatoes and season with salt and freshly ground black pepper. Cover with a lid and bring to the boil.

3 Once boiling, the dish can be simmered over the coals, so pull a few coals out to the edge and surround the dish. Cook for about 30 minutes, topping up with hot coals as necessary and ensuring that the curry keeps simmering gently. Add the potatoes and cook for a further 30 minutes, stirring occasionally, until tender.

4 The curry is ready when the pumpkin has melted into the dish and thickened it, but the potatoes should retain their texture and shape. If you want to cook this dish for longer, that's fine, but just don't add the potatoes until the final 30 minutes of cooking. Check the seasoning and adjust as desired, then serve in bowls.

LEFTOVER FRIED-RICE

This meal is just what it says it is! I often make this for our final camp lunch or dinner as you can use up any leftovers from previous meals or the one or two vegetables that are still lurking in the cooler. I've given suggestions, but so long as you've got the rice, you can add whatever you like.

SERVES 4

200 g (1 cup) raw basmati rice or 500–600 g (3½ cups) cooked rice
2 tablespoons vegetable oil
2 tablespoons soy sauce
3 eggs, lightly beaten
cooked boneless meat, such as chicken, sausages, beef or lamb, shredded or diced (even some bacon slices would be tasty)
cooked chopped vegetables, such as carrots, winter squash or snow peas
2 cooked corn cobs, kernels removed, or 420 g (15 oz) can sweet corn, drained
sweet chilli sauce, to serve (optional)

1. If preparing the rice from scratch, cook according to the packet instructions. Drain well and leave to cool, using a fork to fluff up the grains occasionally. You can cook this earlier in the day if you like and store in the cooler.

2. Heat the oil in a large frying pan or wok. This is best done over a gas cooker, but it will work well over a fire too. Combine the soy sauce and egg in a bowl, then pour into the pan and swirl around. Sit for about 40 seconds, then stir around to mix up and lightly scramble.

3. Once the egg is almost cooked, add the cooled rice and stir well to combine. Then add any meat and vegetables you are using and mix everything together well.

4. Season with salt and freshly ground black pepper, (remembering that the soy sauce is salty) and cook, stirring regularly for about 5 minutes, or until it is piping hot.

5. Remove from the heat and set aside for a couple of minutes to let the flavours mingle, Serve the rice accompanied by sweet chilli sauce, if desired.

To remove corn kernels from the cob, sit the cobs upright on a board, then use a sharp knife to slice as close to the cob as possible.

> *Do not expect the chicken to go golden brown while cooking. However, you will end up with a very tender, moist chicken.*

ONE-POT ROAST CHICKEN WITH VEGETABLES

This dish couldn't really be any simpler – chop your vegies, put them in a casserole dish, top with a whole chicken, then leave it to cook over the fire while you sit back and enjoy the afternoon. If you're anything like my family, it will give you the chance to get everyone involved in a spontaneous game of baseball. When the game is over, dinner for your ravenous team is ready and waiting.

SERVES 4

80 ml (⅓ cup) olive oil or vegetable oil

3 large floury potatoes, cut into 3 cm (1¼ in) chunks

4 carrots, cut into 3 cm (1¼ in) chunks

1 red onion, cut into 8 wedges

4 garlic cloves, peeled and squashed with the back of a blunt knife

1.5 kg (3½ lb) whole chicken, preferably free-range

steamed green vegetables or a salad, to serve (optional)

1 Heat 60 ml (¼ cup) of the oil in a large camp oven or casserole dish on a grill rack over the fire. Once the oil is hot, add the potato, carrot, onion and 2 of the garlic cloves. Season with salt and freshly ground black pepper and stir to coat the vegetables in the oil.

2 Put the remaining squashed garlic inside the chicken, then drizzle or brush the outside of the chicken with the remaining oil and season with salt and pepper. Use a sharp knife to make two slits in each thigh to help it cook evenly.

3 Sit the chicken among the vegetables, moving the vegetables to surround it if necessary, and cover with a lid. Sit the dish to the side of the fire or in the coals away from the direct heat, cover, and cook for 1½–2 hours, or until the vegetables and chicken are tender. You will need to stir occasionally to prevent the vegetables on the bottom from burning. Check the chicken is ready by piercing the thigh, the juices should run clear when cooked.

4 Remove from the fire and let it sit, covered, for 5 minutes. Carefully remove the chicken from the dish, tipping any juices back into the dish. Carve the chicken and serve with the vegetables from the dish and steamed greens or a salad on the side.

HEARTY BEAN AND VEGETABLE 'STOUP'

We go camping throughout winter as well as summer, although I have to admit that even we draw the line at camping when we know it's going to rain. This dish is brilliant whatever the weather – the name says it all really – it is a cross between a stew and a soup, hence the name our family has given to this 'stoup'!

SERVES 4

2 tablespoons olive oil or vegetable oil
1 onion, chopped
2 garlic cloves, roughly chopped
1 large leek, sliced
2 carrots, peeled and sliced
3 large potatoes, cut into small chunks
400 g (14 oz) can cannellini or kidney beans, rinsed and drained
400 g (14 oz) can diced tomatoes
crusty bread or damper (*see* pages 144–48), to serve
grated parmesan or tasty cheese, to serve (optional)

1   Heat the oil in a large saucepan or camp oven on a grill rack over the fire or a gas cooker. Add the onion, garlic and leek and cook, stirring regularly for about 10 minutes. If it gets too hot, add a dash of water to the pan to cool it down.

2   Add the carrot and potato to the pan and stir well to combine. Add the beans and tomatoes, then add 1½ cans of water (using the tomato can) and stir gently. Season with salt and freshly ground black pepper, ensure all the vegetables are submerged, then cover and return to the boil.

3   Once boiling, move the pan to the side of the fire or surround by hot coals away from direct heat and cook for about 35 minutes, or until the vegetables are tender. You may need to replace the coals every so often to keep it simmering. It's okay to let this dish sit for a while – it will become a bit mushy but the flavour will be great.

4   Check the seasoning and adjust as desired, then divide the soup between bowls and serve with crusty bread or damper. It also tastes great with a little grated cheese on top.

A couple of chopped bacon slices thrown in with the onion makes a tasty addition to this dish.

ROAST PORK WITH VEGETABLES

I prefer to cook this dish with a joint that still has the bone in, as it gives it more flavour. However, you can easily use a boned joint, just cook it for about 30 minutes less. See if your butcher will remove the skin and fat for you and then vacuum pack it (they may charge extra for this). This will save you some time at the campsite and avoid making it too messy.

SERVES 4

60 ml (¼ cup) olive oil
2 onions, thickly sliced
2 teaspoons sea salt
4 large potatoes, cut into
  1 cm (½ in) thick slices
1.8 kg (4 lb) pork leg, bone in,
  skin and fat removed
2–3 carrots, cut into chunks
1 tablespoon wholegrain
  mustard
185 ml (¾ cup) beer or apple
  juice

1 Drizzle about 1½ tablespoons of the oil into a camp oven or a large heavy-based saucepan and arrange the onions in a layer in the base of the pan. Season with salt and freshly ground black pepper and drizzle with a little more oil, then add a layer of potatoes.

2 Sit the pork on top and arrange the carrot around the meat. Drizzle the pork with the remaining oil and season. Cover the pan and sit on a grill rack over the fire for about 2 hours, checking the temperature occasionally and stirring everything around. Roast until the pork is almost cooked through – check by slicing close to the bone, it should still be a little pink and look a bit watery.

3 Meanwhile, combine the mustard and beer or apple juice in a bowl, stirring well.

4 After about 2 hours, pour the mustard and beer mixture into the dish and stir well, scraping the base and sides of the pan to remove any delicious bits that are stuck to the pan. Cook for a further 30 minutes, or until the pork is tender. Do not overcook or the meat will become dry.

5 Remove the pork from the pan, cut into slices and remove and discard the bone. Return the pork to the pan with the vegetables and serve immediately.

PASTA, BEAN AND VEGETABLE STEW

This is like the Italian dish 'pasta e fagioli', a simple broth of pasta and beans, to which I've added extra vegetables and a good dollop of pesto at the end to give it a boost of flavour. My husband insists that it be served with crusty bread, although it's not essential, as the stew already has both pasta and beans in it.

SERVES 4–6

2–3 tablespoons olive oil
1 large onion, halved and thinly sliced
3 garlic cloves, roughly chopped
2 zucchini, halved lengthwise, then sliced widthwise
1 red capsicum (bell pepper), seeded and diced
2 x 400 g (14 oz) cans kidney beans, rinsed and drained
200 g (2 cups) small pasta shapes
1.25 litres (5 cups) chicken or vegetable stock or water (or a mixture of both)
3 tablespoons pesto
50 g (½ cup firmly packed) finely grated parmesan cheese
crusty bread, to serve (optional)

1 Heat the olive oil in a camp oven or a large heavy-based saucepan on a grill rack over the fire or a gas cooker. Add the onion and garlic and cook for 5–10 minutes, stirring occasionally.

2 Add the zucchini and bell pepper, stir to combine, and cook for 3–4 minutes, or until the zucchini is just starting to brown.

3 Add the beans, pasta and stock or water, season with salt and freshly ground black pepper, then cover and bring to the boil. Move to the side of the fire and simmer gently for about 15 minutes, or until the pasta is cooked.

4 Just before serving the stew, stir in the pesto, divide between bowls and sprinkle with parmesan cheese.

Don't forget the pesto and canned beans.

BARLEY 'RISOTTO' WITH BUTTERNUT SQUASH

Barley makes a great risotto-style dish, but doesn't need stirring like risotto rice. For added creaminess, I sometimes add cream cheese at the end, but it's not essential. However, cream cheese is a useful ingredient to have while camping, as it can be used as a sandwich filling or added to pasta sauces.

SERVES 4

2 tablespoons olive oil
1 onion, chopped
2 garlic cloves, crushed
450 g (3 cups) chopped butternut or other creamy winter squash
300 g (1½ cups) pearl barley
750 ml (3 cups) vegetable or chicken stock or water
140 g (1 cup) peas
40 g cream cheese (optional)
mixed salad or steamed green vegetables, to serve (optional)

1 Heat the olive oil in a deep-sided heavy-based frying pan or camp oven on a grill rack over the fire or a gas cooker. Add the onion, garlic and pumpkin and cook gently, covered, for about 10 minutes, stirring occasionally.

2 Add the barley and stir to coat well in the onion mixture. Add the stock and stir to combine. Cover with a lid and bring to the boil.

3 Once boiling, if you are cooking over the fire, move the pan to a cooler part of the fire away from direct heat. Cover and simmer for about 1 hour, stirring occasionally until the barley is tender. Check the liquid level after 40 minutes – if it looks dry add 60–80 ml (¼–⅓ cup) water. Mash the squash into the barley a little at this stage. Add the peas and cook for a further 5 minutes.

4 When the barley is cooked it will still have a definite bite, it shouldn't soften completely. Season with salt and freshly ground black pepper as required, remembering if using stock it may be quite salty. Stir in the cream cheese, if using, and serve with a salad or steamed green vegetables.

Chop the pumpkin into 2 cm (¾ in) pieces. It should break down into the risotto as it cooks, to both thicken the 'risotto' and flavour it.

Don't forget the dried oregano.

ONE-POT LAMB SHOULDER WITH WHITE BEANS AND TOMATO SAUCE

There are a couple of optional ingredients in this recipe – it's up to you if you add them. The feta is a salty, creamy addition that softens the tomato sauce flavour, while the olives are there just because I love black olives!

SERVES 4–6

2 tablespoons olive oil
1 large onion, halved and sliced
2 garlic cloves, chopped
1.2–1.4 kg (2¾–3 lb) boneless shoulder of lamb
375 ml (1½ cups) red wine
2 x 400 g (14 oz) cans diced tomatoes
1 teaspoon dried oregano
2 x 400 g (14 oz) cans cannellini beans, rinsed and drained
about 20 pitted kalamata olives (optional)
200 g (7 oz) feta cheese, crumbled, to serve (optional)
crusty bread, to serve
steamed green beans or other vegetables, to serve

1 Heat the oil in a camp oven or large heavy-based saucepan on a grill rack over the fire. Add the onion and garlic and cook for about 10 minutes, stirring regularly, or until light golden.

2 Add the lamb and cook for about 10 minutes, turning the lamb to brown on all sides. Add 125 ml (½ cup) of the red wine, then add the tomatoes and oregano. Season with salt and freshly ground black pepper, cover, and bring to the boil.

3 Move the dish to the side of the fire or surround by coals away from direct heat, cover, and cook for 2 hours. Check the dish occasionally and gradually add the remaining 250 ml (1 cup) wine (or a bit more if you like!), making sure there is still plenty of sauce – if not add a little extra water. If cooking over coals, turn the pan every 15 minutes to ensure it keeps simmering gently and cooks evenly.

4 Add the cannellini beans and olives, if using, and cook for a further 30 minutes, or until the lamb is very tender.

5 Remove the meat and break it into bite-sized pieces, then return to the pan with the vegetables, scatter over the feta, if using, and divide between bowls. Serve with crusty bread and steamed greens.

POT-ROASTED PORK
WITH POTATOES AND PEARS

This tasty pork dish is very quick to put together and once it's cooking on the fire, you can sit back and relax while the pork simmers gently. The end result is meltingly tender pork with soft potatoes and fruit. It might sound a little gourmet to some people but don't let that worry you – it's just simple, camping gourmet! Apples can easily be used in place of the pears.

SERVES 4–6

1 kg (2¼ lb) strip loin pork, skin and fat removed, cut into 2 cm (¾ in) cubes
3 medium (about 500 g/1 lb) floury potatoes, cut into chunks
4 pears (unpeeled), cored and quartered
500 ml (2 cups) water, chicken or vegetable stock
125 ml (½ cup) beer (optional)
140 g (1 cup) peas
green vegetables, crusty bread or damper (*see* pages 144–48), to serve

1   Put the pork, potato and pear into a camp oven or large heavy-based saucepan and toss to combine. Season with salt and freshly ground black pepper.

2   Pour over the water or stock and the beer, adding an extra 125 ml (½ cup) water if not using the beer.

3   Sit the dish to the side of the fire or surrounded by coals away from direct heat, cover, and cook for 2½–3 hours, adding extra hot coals as necessary to ensure that the curry is always simmering gently. Stir occasionally and be careful not to overcook the pork.

4   Add the peas and cook for a further 5 minutes. Divide the pork and pears between bowls and serve with green vegetables, crusty bread or damper.

To save time and mess at the campsite prepare the pork at home before you go. Remove the skin and fat and chop it into cubes, then pack it in an airtight container and keep in the cooler until needed.

SALADS, BIG AND SMALL

In hotter weather you might not feel like cooking much after a day of adventuring around the campsite or further afield, but it's still good to have a substantial and healthy meal. Whether served alongside grilled meats or fish, or on their own, these salads are perfect for total fire-ban days. Keep in mind that salad leaves won't last very long, so bring whole lettuces instead, ensuring they don't get squashed at the bottom of the cooler. Alternatively, you can wash salad leaves before you set off and pack into airtight containers to give them a longer life.

One of my favourite meals in this chapter is the soba noodle and smoked fish salad. Smoked fish is a great option for camping because, unlike fresh fish, it will last for several days in the cooler. Some of these recipes, such as the hearty sausage salad, are useful for adapting leftovers, but can also be cooked from scratch.

SOBA NOODLE
AND SMOKED FISH SALAD

Even though smoked fish has a longer shelf life than fresh, it must still be stored in the cooler. Celery adds a bit of crunch to this salad – any leftover stalks can be added to campfire soups or stews. The pickled ginger in this dish is optional, but it really enhances the flavour, so it's definitely worth getting hold of some if you can.

SERVES 4

270 g (9½ oz) packet
   soba noodles
200 g (½ lb) smoked fish,
   such as salmon, trout
   or mackerel
½ small red onion,
   thinly sliced
3 tablespoons toasted
   pine nuts
2 celery stalks, thinly sliced
1–2 tablespoons pickled
   ginger, roughly chopped

LEMON DRESSING
60 ml (¼ cup) light olive oil
juice of ½ lemon

1. Cook the soba noodles in boiling water for 4 minutes, or according to the packet instructions. Drain, return to the pan, and pour cold water over them to halt the cooking process. Leave for 2 minutes to cool, then drain and place in a large serving bowl.

2. Break the fish into bite-sized pieces and add to the noodles with the onion, toasted pine nuts, celery and pickled ginger.

3. Combine the lemon dressing ingredients in a small bowl and season with salt and freshly ground black pepper. Pour over the salad and toss well to combine. This dish will happily sit (out of the sun) for an hour or so before serving.

Soba noodles are Japanese buckwheat noodles. They are great in soups or salads. If you can't find toasted pine nuts, toast some in a dry frying pan for 1–2 minutes.

PASTA SALAD WITH BACON, AVOCADO, ARUGULA AND CHERRY TOMATOES

This is a great way to use up any leftover cooked pasta. Different pasta shapes can be combined together, so you can use up any boxes you may have lying around the campsite that haven't been finished off. If you know you're going to be making this for lunch or dinner, cook extra bacon at breakfast and store it in your cooler.

SERVES 4

600–700 g (1¼–1½ lb) cold cooked pasta (or 300 g/10½ oz dried pasta cooked, drained and cooled)

6 middle bacon slices, cooked until crisp, then roughly chopped

2 avocados, pits removed, flesh diced

250 g (9 oz) cherry tomatoes, quartered

2 handfuls of rocket (arugula) or other salad leaves

BALSAMIC CHILLI DRESSING

60 ml (¼ cup) olive oil

1 tablespoon balsamic or white wine vinegar

1 red chilli, seeded and finely diced (optional)

1 Put the cooked pasta in a large bowl. Add the bacon, avocado, tomato and arugula and mix well.

2 Combine the balsamic chilli dressing ingredients in a small bowl and season with salt and freshly ground black pepper. Pour over the salad and toss to coat – if you have time, leave for about 20 minutes to allow all the flavours to mingle, before serving.

SMOKED CHICKEN AND POTATO SALAD WITH CAPER AND MUSTARD MAYONNAISE

Smoked chicken is useful to take camping as the smoking process prolongs its use-by date. However, you can also use leftover cooked chicken. If you don't have any salad leaves to serve with this, don't worry it will still taste delicious.

SERVES 4

500–600 g (1–1⅓ lb, about 20) small waxy potatoes, such as new potatoes, larger ones halved or quartered
1 kg (2¼ lb) whole smoked chicken, or about 450–500 g (1 pound) cooked chicken, skin and bones discarded, meat shredded
4 spring onions (scallions), finely chopped
2 handfuls of salad leaves (optional)

CAPER AND MUSTARD MAYONNAISE
1 tablespoon capers, finely chopped
120 g (½ cup) good-quality, whole egg mayonnaise
2 teaspoons wholegrain mustard
juice of ½ lemon

1 Cook the potatoes in salted water for about 20 minutes, or until tender all the way through when pierced with the point of a sharp knife. Drain well and set aside to cool slightly.

2 Meanwhile, combine all of the ingredients for the caper and mustard mayonnaise in a small bowl and season with salt and freshly ground black pepper.

3 Pour the mayonnaise over the still-warm potatoes and mix well to combine. If you have time, set aside for 30 minutes to allow the flavours to develop.

4 Add the chicken and onion to the potato and gently combine. Serve the salad on a bed of salad leaves, if using.

Don't forget the dressing ingredients.

PASTA SALAD
WITH ROASTED VEGETABLES

This is a filling salad, great for sharing after a busy day at the beach or when you are tired and hungry after a hike. This salad can also be packed up and taken with you as a picnic. I'm not sure why – maybe it's the pesto dressing – but I find that kids who often don't like vegetables are happy to munch away on this dish.

SERVES 4

300 g (10½ oz) dried pasta
2 tablespoons olive oil
12 brown or button
   mushrooms
2 large zucchini
200 g (1 cup) jar roasted
   red capsicum (peppers),
   roughly chopped
340 g (12 oz) artichoke
   hearts in olive oil, drained
   and chopped
16 pitted kalamata olives
   (optional)

PESTO DRESSING
1 tablespoon pesto
2 tablespoons olive oil
2 tablespoons lemon juice

1 Cook the pasta in a saucepan of boiling water according to the box instructions. Drain well and place in a large serving bowl.

2 Combine the pesto dressing ingredients in a small bowl, then pour over the warm pasta and mix well. Set aside.

3 Put the olive oil in a bowl and season with salt and freshly ground black pepper. Toss the mushrooms in the oil and cook on a barbecue flatplate or in a frying pan over the fire for about 5 minutes, turning once or twice so they cook evenly.

4 Halve the zucchini to make two shorter pieces, then cut into long slices about 5 mm thick and coat in the seasoned oil. Cook for about 2 minutes, then turn over and cook until soft.

5 Once cooked, chop the mushrooms and zucchini into bite-sized pieces and add to the pasta with the bell pepper, artichoke and olives. Mix everything together well and serve warm or cold.

Don't forget the pre-bought jars of vegetables and pesto.

HEARTY SAUSAGE SALAD

There's bound to be some sausages (or lamb chops) left over from one of your campsite meals and this is the perfect recipe to use them up. Keep them in the cooler until you're ready to throw this quick and filling salad together. It can be made with either cooked pasta or potatoes, or you can use a combination of both. Quantities given are just a rough suggestion – the beauty of this dish is that it copes well with spontaneous improvisation.

SERVES 4

300 g (10½ oz) dried pasta or 6 potatoes, roughly chopped
6–8 cooked sausages or lamb chops, sliced or meat roughly chopped
450 g (15 oz) can beets, chopped
180 g mozzarella, quartered, or feta cheese, crumbled (optional)

MAYONNAISE DRESSING
80 ml (⅓ cup) good-quality whole-egg mayonnaise
1 tablespoon white wine vinegar or lemon juice
1 tablespoon wholegrain mustard

1 If cooking pasta from scratch, put in a saucepan of salted boiling water and cook according to the box instructions. If using potatoes, place in a saucepan and cover with water. Bring to the boil and cook for about 15–20 minutes, or until tender when pierced with the point of a sharp knife. Drain the pasta or potatoes and transfer to a large bowl.

2 Meanwhile, make the mayonnaise dressing. Combine all of the ingredients in a small bowl and season with salt and freshly ground black pepper. Add 2 tablespoons of water to thin it slightly. If you have made the pasta or potato from scratch, pour the dressing over while still warm and mix well to coat. If you have time, leave the dressing to soak in until the pasta or potato has cooled.

3 Add the sausages or lamb, beets and fresh mozzarella or feta cheese and stir to gently combine until you have a beautiful light pink salad!

Roast fresh beets and peel before you leave home. It can be stored in the cooler for two to three days.

EGG SALAD ON CRUSTY TOASTS

I suppose this dish isn't technically a salad, but it makes a satisfying brunch or lunch just the same. If you have fussy members of the family, tailor the topping to suit — you can leave out the corn and serve the avocado separately, if desired.

SERVES 4

6 eggs
4–6 middle bacon slices
1 large avocado, pit removed, flesh chopped
420 g (15 oz) can sweet corn kernels, drained or 2 corn cobs, kernels removed
8–12 thick slices crusty bread
olive oil, for brushing
1 garlic clove, halved

LEMON CAPER DRESSING
80 ml (⅓ cup) good-quality whole-egg mayonnaise
1 tablespoon lemon juice
2 teaspoons capers, finely chopped (optional)

Don't forget a crusty loaf of bread.

1 Put the eggs into a saucepan of boiling water and cook for 7 minutes, or until hard-boiled. Drain, cool in cold water, then peel and place into a large bowl. Roughly mash.

2 Cook the bacon in a frying pan until just crispy. Drain on paper towel, then cut into small pieces and add to the eggs with the avocado and sweet corn.

3 Combine the lemon caper dressing ingredients in a small bowl and season with salt and freshly ground black pepper. Add to the egg mixture and gently combine.

4 Brush the bread with olive oil and rub with the cut side of a garlic clove. Toast over a fire or in a frying pan on a gas cooker until lightly toasted.

5 Spoon some egg and avocado mixture onto each slice of toast and serve warm.

TUNA AND BEAN SALAD

This is the perfect summer salad – it is quick and easy to prepare and it doesn't require cooking. It is a great choice for those days when you can't or don't want to light a fire or turn on the gas.

SERVES 4

1 romaine lettuce, leaves separated and roughly torn
425 g (15 oz) can tuna in spring water, drained
400 g (14 oz) can kidney beans, rinsed and drained
400 g (14 oz) cannellini beans, rinsed and drained
250 g (9 oz) cherry tomatoes, halved
1 red capsicum (bell pepper), seeded and roughly chopped
½ red onion, thinly sliced

VINEGAR AND HERB DRESSING
60 ml (¼ cup) olive oil
1 tablespoon white wine vinegar
1 teaspoon dried oregano

1 Put the lettuce leaves in a large bowl then add all of the remaining salad ingredients and toss gently to combine.

2 Combine the vinegar and herb dressing ingredients in a small bowl and season well with salt and freshly ground black pepper.

3 Pour the dressing over the salad and serve. If making this in advance, don't add the dressing until the last minute or the lettuce leaves will wilt.

Don't forget the dried oregano.

THAI BEEF SALAD WITH NOODLES

This recipe can be cooked over a gas cooker, an open fire or on a barbecue. Make it as spicy or as mild as you like. If you prefer it mild, leave out the red chilli, but keep the sweet chilli sauce. One of my kids adores plain noodles, so if you have anyone like this in your family keep some noodles and vegetables separate to serve with the beef.

SERVES 4

250 g (9 oz packet) rice
  vermicelli noodles
600 g (1⅓ lb) beef
  fillet steaks
olive oil or vegetable oil,
  for brushing
juice of 1 lime
1 red chilli, seeded and
  finely chopped (optional)
60 ml (¼ cup) sweet
  chilli sauce
1 tablespoon fish sauce
250 g (9 oz) cherry tomatoes,
  halved or quartered
2 Lebanese (short)
  cucumbers, diced

Don't forget the sweet chilli and fish sauces.

1 Soak the noodles in a bowl of boiling water for about 4 minutes, or according to the packet instructions, then drain. Sit in a bowl of cold water for a couple of minutes to cool, then drain again. Place into a large bowl.

2 Brush the beef steaks with oil on both sides and season with salt and freshly ground black pepper.

3 Cook the beef on a barbecue, over the fire or in a frying pan on a gas cooker for about 3 minutes, then turn over and cook for a further 2 minutes. This is the approximate timing for a steak about 2 cm (¾ in) thick, cooked to medium–rare. Adjust the cooking time according to the thickness of your steak and how you prefer it. Cover and set aside while you make the salad.

4 Combine the lime juice, chilli, sweet chilli and fish sauces. Pour over the noodles and toss to coat. Add the tomato and cucumber and toss to combine.

5 To serve, thinly slice the steak and arrange on top of the salad.

Don't forget the dried oregano and a loaf of crusty bread.

CHARGRILLED LAMB WITH HALOUMI, OLIVES AND LEMON

Drawing on the flavours of Greece, this salad is always popular. Cooking the lamb over the fire gives it a delicious smoky flavour. Ask your butcher to bone out a loin of lamb to give you backstrap and fillet. This is much cheaper than just asking for lamb fillet or buying it at the supermarket. One lemon should provide enough juice for the lamb and the dressing.

SERVES 4

1 tablespoon olive oil
2 garlic cloves, crushed
1 teaspoon dried oregano
1 tablespoon lemon juice
600 g (1⅓ lb) lamb fillet
3 firm, ripe tomatoes, roughly chopped
16 pitted kalamata olives
2 tablespoons capers, roughly chopped
1 large handful of arugula leaves (optional)
250 g (8 oz packge) haloumi cheese or queso blanco, cut into 1 cm (½ in) thick slices widthwise
crusty bread, to serve

LEMON AND HERB DRESSING
2 tablespoons olive oil
1 tablespoon lemon juice
1 teaspoon dried oregano

1 Combine the olive oil, garlic, oregano and lemon juice in a shallow container. Season with salt and freshly ground black pepper. Add the lamb and turn to coat in the marinade. Set aside in the cooler for 30 minutes. This isn't essential, but it will enhance the flavour.

2 Remove the lamb from the marinade (reserving the marinade) and pat the lamb dry with a paper towel.

3 Cook the lamb on a barbecue hotplate or on a grill rack over the fire for about 2 minutes on each side, or until seared on the outside and medium–rare on the inside. The exact timing will depend on the thickness of the meat. Set aside for 5 minutes to rest, then cut the lamb into thin slices.

4 Combine the lamb, tomato, olives, capers and arugula, if using, in a large bowl. Combine the lemon and herb dressing ingredients in a separate small bowl and drizzle over the lamb, tossing to combine.

5 Dunk both sides of the haloumi into the reserved marinade. Cook for 1–2 minutes on each side until golden.

6 Top the salad with the haloumi and serve soon after cooking, or the haloumi will become rubbery. Serve with crusty bread for mopping up all the delicious juices.

CHICKPEA, FETA AND TOMATO SALAD

I came up with this salad after finding a block of feta in the fridge just before we were going camping one very hot summer weekend. I thought a Middle Eastern inspired salad would be ideal, as it requires no cooking. To make this salad even more substantial, add some toasted pita triangles. For variation you can try adding pitted kalamata olives and capers.

SERVES 4

400 g (14 oz) can chickpeas, rinsed and drained
200 g (7 oz) feta cheese, crumbled or diced
250 g (9 oz) cherry tomatoes, halved
1 green capsicum (bell pepper), seeded and sliced
1 small red onion, halved and thinly sliced
2 short cucumbers, diced
3 small or 2 large pita breads (optional)

TANGY DRESSING

60 ml (¼ cup) olive oil
¼ teaspoon chilli powder
2 tablespoons red wine vinegar or lemon juice

1   Combine the chickpeas, feta, tomato, bell pepper, onion and cucumber in a shallow serving dish.

2   If you want to add the pita triangles, prepare them now. If you have a fire going, toast the pita bread briefly on each side. Alternatively, toast in a frying pan on a gas cooker. Cut into small triangles then leave to crisp up.

3   Combine the tangy dressing ingredients in a small bowl and season with salt and freshly ground black pepper. Pour over the salad.

4   Arrange the pita triangles on top, if using, and serve.

Don't forget the chilli powder and red wine vinegar.

CHARGRILLED ZUCCHINI, ONION AND FETA SALAD

I love chargilled vegetables, so if we've got a fire going, I always like to throw some on, then I think about what else I can add to create a complete meal. It's also great served alongside meat or fish dishes. The salad leaves are entirely optional, add some if you have any available.

SERVES 4
as an accompaniment

80 ml (⅓ cup) olive oil
2 tablespoon balsamic vinegar
3 zucchini, cut lengthwise into thin slices
2 red or brown onions, cut into thin wedges
1 teaspoon dried oregano
1 large handful salad leaves (optional)
200 g (7 oz) feta cheese, crumbled

Don't forget the dried oregano.

1 To make the dressing, combine the olive oil and balsamic vinegar in a small bowl and season well with salt and freshly ground black pepper.

2 Put the zucchini on a plate and spoon over about 1 tablespoon of the dressing, turn to coat, then place on a medium–hot barbecue flatplate or grill rack over the fire. Repeat with the onion wedges and place over the heat. Cook the vegetables for 8–10 minutes, turning regularly until softened and starting to blacken.

3 Remove the vegetables from the heat and set aside to cool. Meanwhile, whisk the oregano into the remaining dressing.

4 Once the vegetables have cooled, toss together with the salad leaves, if using. Scatter the feta cheese over the vegetables, drizzle with the dressing and serve.

COLOURFUL TOMATO AND MOZZARELLA SALAD WITH BALSAMIC DRESSING

Not only is this salad packed full of flavour but it looks beautiful too. Try this at the height of summer when tomatoes are at their best and you can find a variety of colours and sizes. This salad will sit quite happily for an hour or so in the cooler, during which time the flavours will develop.

SERVES 4–6
as an accompaniment

60 ml (¼ cup) olive oil
1 tablespoon balsamic
   vinegar
250 g (9 oz) red cherry
   tomatoes, halved
250 g (9 oz) yellow or orange
   cherry tomatoes, halved
2 firm, ripe tomatoes,
   roughly chopped
180 g (6½ oz) mozzarella,
   halved or quartered
1 small handful fresh basil
   leaves, roughly torn
   (optional)

1 Combine the olive oil and balsamic vinegar in a small bowl and season with salt and freshly ground black pepper.

2 Combine all of the tomatoes in a serving dish with the mozzarella and drizzle over the dressing, tossing gently to combine.

3 Scatter over the basil, if using, and serve.

Look for bocconcini, which are baby mozzarella, ideal for salads.

CRUNCHY ROMAINE AND RADISH SALAD

Although I love simple leafy salads, sometimes I really crave a bit of crunch and that's how this salad came about – the radishes also a wonderful peppery flavour that I adore.

SERVES 4
as an accompaniment

2 heads of romaine, outer leaves discarded
1 bunch radishes, trimmed and sliced or chopped
2 short cucumbers, diced
3 scallions, thinly sliced

MUSTARD DRESSING
60 ml (¼ cup) olive oil
1½ tablespoons red wine vinegar
2 teaspoons wholegrain mustard

1 Separate and wash the lettuce leaves and shake them dry. Place in a serving bowl, roughly tearing them as you go. Scatter over the radish, cucumber and scallions.

2 To make the mustard dressing, combine the olive oil, vinegar and mustard and season with salt and freshly ground black pepper. Pour over the salad and toss well before serving.

Don't forget the red wine vinegar and mustard.

GREEN SALAD WITH LEMON AND MUSTARD MAYONNAISE DRESSING

The beauty of this salad is its simplicity – a few well chosen, good-quality ingredients thrown together to make a side dish that goes well with a multitude of meat and fish dishes. This is especially good with the quick fish kebabs (page 40) or the marinated butterflied leg of lamb (page 55).

SERVES 4
as an accompaniment

1 head romaine lettuce
1 large handful rocket (arugula) leaves
1 large short cucumber, diced
1 avocado, pit removed, flesh diced (optional)

LEMON AND MUSTARD MAYONNAISE DRESSING
3 tablespoons good-quality mayonnaise
1½ tablespoons lemon juice
1 tablespoon wholegrain or Dijon mustard

1 Combine the romaine and arugula in a bowl, tearing any large leaves. Add the cucumber and avocado, if using, and toss gently to combine.

2 To make the lemon and mustard mayonnaise dressing, combine the mayonnaise, lemon juice and mustard, adding 2 teaspoons of water to thin it out. Season with salt and freshly ground black pepper.

3 Drizzle the dressing over the salad and serve. Do not dress the salad too far in advance or the leaves will wilt.

Don't forget the mayonnaise and mustard.

LENTIL, FETA AND TOMATO SALAD

Cans of lentils are useful on camping trips for adding interest to salads. I often take some with us in the height of summer when total fire bans may be in place and we can't light fires.

SERVES 4
as an accompaniment

400 g (14 oz) can lentils, drained
200 g (7 oz) feta cheese, crumbled or cubed
1 short cucumber, diced
250 g (9 oz) cherry tomatoes, halved or quartered if large
60 ml (¼ cup) olive oil
juice of ½ lemon

1 It is preferable (but not essential) to rinse the lentils, as the liquid in the can sometimes makes the lentils taste metallic. If you have a sieve, drain them and pour a can or two of water over to rinse off.

2 Place the lentils in a large bowl, add the feta, cucumber and tomato and toss to combine.

3 Combine the olive oil and lemon juice in a small bowl and season well with salt and freshly ground black pepper. Pour over the lentil salad and toss to coat before serving. This salad will sit happily in the cooler for a couple of hours if needed.

If you can't find canned lentils, use beans.

CHARGRILLED CORN, TOMATO AND RADICCHIO SALAD

Radicchio are red-coloured lettuces with a slightly bitter taste, which in this recipe is perfectly offset by the sweetness of the corn. Radicchio is good to take camping because it is usually sold whole, so it will travel and store well. If you can't find any, use a romaine lettuce instead.

SERVES 4
as an accompaniment

80 ml (⅓ cup) olive oil
2 tablespoons red or white
    wine vinegar
a pinch of sugar
1 tablespoon chopped fresh
    herbs, such as parsley,
    coriander (cilantro), chives
    or dill
2 corn cobs
1 head radicchio
3 firm, ripe tomatoes,
    roughly chopped or 250 g
    (9 oz) cherry tomatoes,
    quartered

1 To make the dressing, put the oil and vinegar, some salt and freshly ground black pepper and a pinch of sugar in a small bowl. Whisk to combine. Stir in the herbs, if using.

2 Cook the corn cobs in boiling water for 5 minutes. Drain, then transfer the corn to a barbecue hotplate or on a grill rack over the fire for about 5 minutes, turning regularly until slightly blackened.

3 Carefully slice off the corn kernels by holding the corn upright on a board and slicing down each side.

4 Discard the outer leaves of the raddichio until you are down to the tight, bright red-purple leaves in the centre. Cut the lettuce in half, then roughly shred or tear the leaves into a serving bowl.

5 Add the tomato, corn and dressing and toss gently to combine. Serve quite soon after preparing, otherwise the leaves will wilt. If preparing in advance, don't add the dressing until the last minute.

If you don't have a fire going while you're making this salad, simply slice the kernels off the corn cobs once you've boiled them.

CAMPFIRE COOKING FOR KIDS

When the family is camping, the pressures of everyday life are absent, so there is more time for the kids to help out with the cooking and it really doesn't matter if they make a mess. These simple recipes will keep all levels of young cooks happy, although they will need adult supervision to cook them, especially over a camp fire.

The pita calzone pizzas are heaps of fun to make and can be customised to suit each child's taste. The honey and soy sausages and easy chicken satay will be enjoyed by grown-ups and kids alike. And what better way to spend a morning or afternoon than getting everyone together to ice and decorate their own cupcakes – it will keep them entertained and is a great shared activity for the whole family.

Measure out the flour, sugar and salt before you leave home. Combine in a re-sealable snack bag or airtight container, then all you have to do is add the wet ingredients before cooking.

BREAKFAST PANCAKES

Who doesn't love pancakes for breakfast? This recipe is extra delicious as the batter contains melted butter. Cook a few, then let people start eating them while the rest are cooking, this way you always have a supply of delicious, hot pancakes at the ready.

MAKES 25–30 small pancakes

185 g (1½ cups) all-purpose flour
1½ teaspoons baking powder
¾ teaspoon salt
(for the self-raising flour recipe)
2 tablespoons sugar
2 eggs, lightly beaten
50 g (3½ tablespoons) butter, melted, plus extra for cooking
310 ml (1¼ cups) milk

TOPPINGS
sliced bananas
nutella
honey or maple syrup
berry jam
cooked bacon

1 Combine the flour, sugar and a pinch of salt in a large bowl. Make a well in the centre.

2 Put the eggs, melted butter and most of the milk into the well. Whisk the wet ingredients together briefly, then incorporate the dry ingredients to form a smooth batter. Add extra milk if needed – the batter shouldn't be too runny. Set aside for 20 minutes, this allows the batter to thicken which in turn leads to better textured pancakes.

3 Heat a little extra butter in a frying pan and swirl around to coat the base of the pan. You can cook these over a gas cooker, over the fire or directly on a barbecue. Add spoonfuls of the batter to the pan and cook until bubbles start to appear on the surface, then carefully turn over and cook the other side until golden and cooked through.

4 Keep warm under a tea towel until you have several to serve and continue cooking the remaining mixture, adding extra butter to the pan as needed. Serve with your choice of toppings.

WARM TORTILLA ROLL-UPS

It's often hard to get the kids to stay near our camp as they're always off exploring, but when I tell them they're making their own meals and it's going to be these warm tortilla roll-ups, suddenly their bicycles, large sticks and other games are immediately abandoned and it's all hands on deck! You can experiment with other fillings, such as avocado, halved cherry tomatoes, olives and salami.

MAKES 4 filled tortillas

4 tortillas
80 g (3 oz) sour cream
8 slices Swiss cheese, halved
200 g (⅓ lb) cooked shredded chicken breast, bacon or ham
160 g (6 oz) mild tomato salsa or pasta sauce

Don't forget the aluminium foil.

1 Spread each tortilla with sour cream, then top with slices of cheese, arranging them in a line down the centre.

2 Top with the chicken, bacon or ham, then spoon the tomato salsa along the middle.

3 Carefully roll up the wraps, but do not turn in the ends. Place each tortilla, seam side down, on a large square of foil. Fold in the sides, then roll it up to enclose.

4 If you have a fire going, place the parcels on a camp grill over the fire for 5 minutes, turning once or twice. Alternatively, heat in a frying pan over a gas cooker, turning to cook evenly.

5 Be careful when opening the tortilla roll-ups as the cheese will be hot.

PITA CALZONE PIZZAS

Lots of people make pizza using pita bread, but as well as cooking them in an oven, you can also cook them over a fire or in a frying pan. I tend to make mine more like the folded pizza calzone so there's less worry about the filling slipping off when you try to plate them. This is the perfect snack for kids and they will love making them.

MAKES 4

4 pita bread pockets
400 g (14 oz) jar tomato
   purée or pizza sauce
250–375 g (2–3 cups) grated
   mozzarella cheese

TOPPINGS
chopped ham
sliced mushrooms
halved, pitted kalamata olives
sliced tomatoes
canned pineapple, drained
   and chopped
sliced avocado

1 An adult will need to help kids heat the pita bread pockets. Place them over the fire briefly, turning once so they puff up. Alternatively, put into a frying pan over a gas cooker. Although this step isn't vital it really makes it easier to open up the pita pockets.

2 Once the pita pockets are cool enough to handle, carefully slice or tear each one open around the edge, almost all the way round, but leaving some still attached (scissors are good for this). Open it out so that it is almost flat.

3 Spread one side of the open pocket with sauce, then top with mozzarella cheese and layer over your favourite toppings. Children might enjoy creating patterns or making a funny face using different ingredients for eyes, nose, mouth, beard, hair and so on.

4 Flip over the top to cover and place over the fire or in the pan for 2 minutes to heat the filling. Turn over and cook for a further 1–2 minutes, or until the cheese has melted.

5 Cut each calzone pizza into halves or wedges and serve immediately, taking care because the cheese will be very hot.

CHEESY BEEF BURGERS

Make sure everyone's hands are clean before they start mixing together these really simple burgers. Once the patties have cooked, the kids will enjoy designing their own burger, using slices of cheese, tomato, pickles and salad – or not!

MAKES 8 small burgers

BEEF PATTIES
1 small onion, finely chopped
1 garlic clove, crushed
600 g (1⅓ lb) good-quality
    ground beef
100 g (1 cup) finely grated
    cheddar, tasty or parmesan
    cheese
2 tablespoons olive oil

TO SERVE
8 small burger buns or 16
    slices of bread
tomato sauce (ketchup)
good-quality whole-egg
    mayonnaise
slices of cheese
slices of tomato
slices of pickle or cucumber
salad leaves

1 Put the onion, garlic, beef and cheese into a large bowl and season with salt and freshly ground black pepper. Use your hands to mix everything together well, squishing and mixing the mince until it turns a slightly pink colour. Divide the meat into eight even-sized portions and shape each portion into a patty.

2 Heat the oil in a frying pan on a grill rack over the fire, on a gas cooker, or directly on a campfire grill. Arrange the burgers in a single layer and cook for 3–4 minutes on each side, or until the burgers are cooked through. The cooking time will depend on the thickness of the burgers and the heat of your fire.

3 Briefly toast the buns or bread to warm through, then add a beef patty and your choice of toppings and sauces.

You could also make four large burgers. Cook them for 5–6 minutes on each side.

BEEF OR CHICKEN KEBABS

You can make these kebabs using either chicken or beef. Although chicken thigh meat takes longer to cook, it stays moister than breast meat when grilled. Use a tender cut of beef, such as fillet. There are lots of filling suggestions, let the kids put them out on a serving platter and choose what they like. If using wooden skewers, soak them in water for 20 minutes before using to prevent them burning during cooking.

MAKES 8 kebabs

2 tablespoons olive oil
2 tablespoons honey
2 tablespoons wholegrain
   mustard
700–800 g (1½–1¾ pounds)
   skinless, boneless chicken
   thigh or breast fillets, or
   beef fillets, cut into 2 cm
   (¾ in) cubes
8 pita breads

TO SERVE
small cucumbers, halved
   lengthwise and sliced
grated carrot
grated cheese
cherry tomatoes, quartered
sliced avocado
rocket (arugula) leaves

1 Combine the olive oil, honey and mustard in a large bowl to make a marinade. Add the chicken or beef pieces to the bowl and mix well to coat the meat. If you have time, set aside in the cooler for 1 hour to let the flavours develop.

2 Thread the meat onto metal skewers, so each cube of meat is just touching, but not too tightly packed.

3 Cook the kebabs on a grill rack over the fire or directly on a barbecue for 12–15 minutes, turning regularly. Ensure the chicken is cooked through before serving, although beef can be served a little rare.

4 Sit the pita breads briefly over the fire to warm through and soften. Carefully pull the meat off the skewers and split open each pita bread. Add your choice of fillings, and serve.

Don't forget the metal skewers.

SIMPLE CHICKEN SATAY

In my experience chicken is loved by pretty much every kid on the planet. Thrown together with their other all-time favourite, peanut butter, and you've got a winning combination. Just make sure the kids wash their hands before and after handling raw chicken.

MAKES 8–10 skewers

700 g (1½ lb) skinless, boneless chicken breast or chicken tenders
400 ml (14 oz) can coconut milk
1 tablespoon soy sauce
100 g (⅓ cup) crunchy or smooth peanut butter

1   Cut the chicken into cubes or into long 6 cm (2½ in) strips. Combine about half of the coconut milk with the soy sauce in a large bowl. Add the chicken, toss to coat and leave to marinate for about 20 minutes in the cooler.

2   Thread the chicken onto the skewers and discard the leftover marinade. Place the skewers on an oiled grill rack over a part of the fire that isn't too hot, so the chicken doesn't burn on the outside before it cooks on the inside. Alternatively, you can cook on a barbecue.

3   Cook the chicken for about 10 minutes, or until just cooked through. Do not overcook or it will become dry.

4   When the chicken is almost cooked, heat the remaining coconut milk and the peanut butter in a small saucepan. Place over the fire or a gas cooker and stir regularly until it is bubbling and thickened. Serve the skewers with the warm satay sauce on the side.

CHEESE AND HAM TORTILLA TRIANGLES

Kids will need a hand cooking these tasty little snacks but they are easy and quick to prepare and always popular. Put out a selection of filling ingredients and let everyone choose their own combinations.

MAKES about 20 wedges

10 tortillas
good-quality egg mayonnaise
sweet chutney (optional)

TOPPINGS
250 g (2 cups) grated
   cheddar or tasty cheese
sliced ham or salami
sliced tomato
sliced avocado

1 Spread half of the tortillas with some mayonnaise and a little chutney, if using.

2 Scatter some cheese over the tortilla halves spread with mayonnaise and layer over your preferred toppings. Children might enjoy creating patterns or making a funny face using different ingredients for the eyes, nose, mouth, beard, hair and so on.

3 Place a second tortilla over the filling like a sandwich. Cook in a frying pan or on a campfire grill for about 3 minutes, turning once – the cheese should be slightly melted and the tortillas golden. Cut into wedges and serve.

HONEY AND SOY SAUSAGES

Getting kids involved in cooking at a young age is really important and that doesn't mean just in your home kitchen. Sometimes a bit of quiet time around the campsite is called for, so I often get my kids to whip up this fast and simple recipe.

MAKES 8 sausages
or about 16 chipolatas

2 tablespoons honey
1 tablespoon soy sauce
1 tablespoon wholegrain
   mustard
8 sausages or 16 chipolatas
salad, to serve (optional)
crusty bread, to serve
   (optional)

1 Find a shallow dish, large enough to hold the sausages. Add the honey, soy and mustard to the dish and mix well.

2 Put the sausages in the dish and turn them in the marinade to make sure the sausages are coated. If you have time, set aside for at least 20 minutes in the cooler to marinate.

3 Cook the sausages in a frying pan on a grill rack over the fire or on a gas cooker, turning regularly – the chipolatas will take about 10 minutes and the sausages about 15 minutes to cook through. The exact cooking time will depend on the heat of your fire and the thickness of your sausages.

4 When the sausages are cooked, serve them with salad and bread. Although whenever I cook these, they go as fast as they are cooked and rarely with an accompaniment!

'MESSY' PLATTER

The idea for this dish came from my sister, who regularly creates a campsite mezze platter for the grown-ups. One fateful trip she decided to create a 'messy' platter for the kids. You don't have to include everything, choose your family favourites.

SERVES 4–6

GUACAMOLE
1 large avocado
4 cherry tomatoes, quartered
2 tablespoons mayonnaise

PEANUT BUTTER DIP
4 tablespoons cream cheese
3 tablespoons peanut butter
2–3 teaspoons milk

'MESSY' BITS
cooked honey and soy sausages
   (opposite) or chipolatas
hard-boiled eggs, halved or
   quartered
cucumber and carrot sticks
cubes of cheese
black olives
salad leaves
hummus
pita bread, cut into triangles

1 To make the guacamole, halve the avocado and ask an adult to remove the pit. Peel and roughly chop, then place in a bowl. Add the tomatoes and mayonnaise and combine, mashing it a little, but still leaving it a bit chunky.

2 To make the peanut butter dip, combine the cream cheese and peanut butter in a bowl. Add the little milk, a little at a time, to soften the mixture slightly, stirring well until smooth.

3 Arrange all of your favourite messy bits on a large platter. You can make a silly face using the ingredients – lettuce for the hair, olives for the eyes, carrot sticks for a moustache and hummus for a beard! Place the guacamole and peanut butter dip on the side and serve.

A BIT OF FUN WITH CUPCAKES

Bake some cupcakes before leaving home. At the campsite make a frosting of cream cheese and jam, then let the kids decorate their cupcakes with sprinkles, chocolate flakes or your preferred toppings. Any leftover frosting is delicious on toast or in sandwiches!

MAKES 12 cupcakes

CUPCAKES
100 g (7 tablespoons) butter, softened
185 g (¾ cup) sugar
½ teaspoon natural vanilla extract
2 eggs
125 ml (½ cup) milk
200 g (1½ cups) all-purpose flour
1½ teaspoons baking powder
¾ teaspoon salt

FROSTING
250 g (9 oz) cream cheese
3 tablespoons strawberry jam

DECORATIONS
sprinkles
chocolate flake, crumbled
mini M&Ms

1 Preheat the oven to 180°C (350°F) and line a standard 12-hole muffin tin with paper liners.

2 Put the butter, sugar and vanilla extract into a bowl and beat with an electric mixer, until pale and soft.

3 Add the eggs, one at a time, and beat until just combined. Mix together the flour, baking soda and salt. Add the milk and flour mixture alternately in small amounts and stir with a wooden spoon until just combined. Do not over-mix.

4 Divide the mixture evenly between the paper liners, then bake for 15–20 minutes, or until cooked and golden on top . Remove from the oven, leave in the tin for 5 minutes, then transfer to a wire rack to cool completely. Store in an airtight container.

AT THE CAMP

5 Beat the cream cheese to soften, then add the jam and mix to combine. Put the different sprinkles and chocolate into separate small bowls. Put the cupcakes out and let the kids decorate them, spreading first with the cream cheese frosting, using a blunt knife, and then adding their favourite toppings. Don't worry about how good they look, let the kids go crazy with the sprinkles.

CAMPFIRE BREAD AND OTHER ESSENTIALS

Campfire bread is very satisfying to cook in an open fire and if you have a camp oven it is simply a matter of mixing three or four basic ingredients together, leaving it to rise for a while, then sitting it in the coals to bake. If you don't have a camp oven, wrap the dough in a double layer of foil and cook surrounded, not on top of, the coals. This chapter includes an easy damper recipe that kids will enjoy cooking, as well as a few variations to suit any occasion.

Similarly, you won't be able to resist the delicious recipe for the French-style pan bagnat, a tasty filled baguette that develops flavour the longer you leave it, making it perfect for taking on a hike. And what campsite meal would be complete without a simple balsamic onion relish that makes the perfect filling for burgers or accompaniment to grilled meat, and the ever-popular quick tomato sauce for serving with pasta.

KIDS' EASY CAMPFIRE DAMPER

Damper is a tried-and-true Australian campfire classic bread that pretty much everyone adores. I like to add butter and sugar, which a traditional damper would not usually include. Let the kids make the dough and divide it into portions, then wrap each portion around the top part of a long stick. The kids can then cook it over the fire. Once cooked, fill the hole where the stick was with honey, jam or nutella. Be warned – once you have made this the first time, your kids will invariably start asking you to make more!

MAKES 6 small breads

300 g (2 cups) all-purpose
   flour, plus extra as needed
1½ teaspoon salt
3 teaspoons baking powder
2 teaspoons sugar
2 tablespoons butter
250–310 ml (1–1¼ cups) milk
honey, jam or nutella,
   to serve

An English scout recently showed me how to make twisted damper – roll your ball of dough into a long sausage shape and wrap this around the top of your stick.

1 Combine the flour, salt, baking powder and sugar in a large bowl. Add the butter and use your fingertips to rub it into the flour until it is all incorporated – it should resemble breadcrumbs.

2 Gradually add the milk and knead to combine, adding just enough to make a dough that isn't too sticky and that can be easily kneaded. If it's too sticky or wet, it will drop off the sticks when it is being cooked. Add a little extra flour if this is the case. Knead in the bowl for about 10 minutes, or until soft and elastic, giving everyone a turn so they all get to join in the fun.

3 Divide the damper into six portions, form into balls and shape into ovals around the top of six long, thick sticks. With parental supervision, let the kids cook the bread over the fire for about 10–15 minutes, turning the bread regularly, until golden brown on all sides. When the bread is cooked, it will sound hollow when tapped. Wait for 5 minutes (if the kids are patient enough), then remove from the stick and fill with your favourite filling.

CHEESE AND HERB CAMPFIRE BREAD

For this bread to work, it's important the beer is at room temperature before you start. If your beer is chilled, pour into a small saucepan and heat gently over the fire or a gas cooker. Don't worry too much if you can't measure things out properly – it is a pretty forgiving recipe.

MAKES 1 loaf

- 450 g (3 cups) all-purpose flour, plus about 2–3 tablespoons extra
- 2 teaspoons salt
- 3 teaspoons baking powder
- 250 ml (1 cup) beer, at room temperature
- 2 tablespoons olive oil
- 75 g (¾ cup) grated cheddar or parmesan cheese
- 3 tablespoons chopped fresh herbs, such as parsley, chives or tarragon, or use 3 teaspoons dried herbs

1 Combine all of the ingredients in a large bowl (preferably a metal one as it will need to sit by the heat at one point) and use your hands to bring the mixture together. If it's sticky, add a little extra flour. Knead in the bowl for about 10 minutes, or until soft and elastic.

2 Cover the dough with a clean tea towel and place close to the fire (but not on it) or in a warm place for 30 minutes, until the dough has risen in size. At the same time, place your camp oven close to the fire to warm through, but don't let it get too hot.

3 Very lightly dust the base of the camp oven with a little extra flour. Transfer the dough to the camp oven, sprinkle lightly with flour, then cover and sit close to the fire surrounded by coals. Don't sit it on top of the coals or the bread will burn. If cooking over a fire pit with a grill tray that swings around, put the camp oven on this and put some coals on top of the camp oven too, to ensure an all-round heat.

4 Cook for 30–40 minutes, checking the coals every now and then, adding more as necessary, until the bread is cooked and it sounds hollow when tapped. If your bread is taking longer to cook, just keep replacing the coals. Remove from the camp oven, leave for 5 minutes, then serve in chunks or slices.

BEER AND PESTO CAMPFIRE BREAD

It's amazing what you can create with so few ingredients. This is such a simple recipe and the addition of beer and pesto raise it from a plain old damper to one that is far more flavourful and interesting. Like all damper, it is delicious for dipping into the juices of casseroles and stews.

MAKES 1 loaf

450 g (3 cups) all-purpose flour, plus about 2–3 tablespoons extra
2 teaspoons salt
3 teaspoons baking powder
250 ml (1 cup) beer, at room temperature
2 tablespoons olive oil
60 g (¼ cup) pesto

This bread can easily be made at home – place it in an ovenproof casserole dish, cover with the lid and bake at 170ºC (340ºF) for about 40 minutes, until it sounds hollow when tapped on the base.

1. Combine all of the ingredients in a large bowl (preferably a metal one as it will need to sit by the heat at one point) and use your hands to bring the mixture together. If it's sticky, add a little extra flour. Knead in the bowl for about 10 minutes, or until soft and elastic.

2. Cover the dough with a clean tea towel and place close to the fire (but not on it) or in a warm place for 30 minutes, until the dough has risen in size. At the same time, place your camp oven close to the fire to warm through, but don't let it get too hot.

3. Very lightly dust the base of the camp oven with a little extra flour. Transfer the dough to the camp oven, sprinkle lightly with flour, then cover and sit close to the fire surrounded by coals. Don't sit it on top of the coals or the bread will burn. If cooking over a fire pit with a grill tray that swings around, put the camp oven on this and put some coals on top of the camp oven too, to ensure an all-round heat.

4. Cook for 30–40 minutes, checking the coals every now and then, adding more as necessary, until the bread is cooked and it sounds hollow when tapped. If your bread is taking longer to cook, just keep replacing the coals. Remove from the camp oven, leave for 5 minutes, then serve in chunks or slices.

SUNDRIED TOMATO AND OLIVE CAMPFIRE BREAD

Of all the bread dampers I make, this is probably my favourite.
When friends try this they are amazed that it is so easy to prepare.
If you have the time, this recipe is definitely worth trying!

MAKES 1 loaf

450 g (3 cups) all-
    purpose flour
2 teaspoons salt
3 teaspoons baking powder
2 tablespoons olive oil
75 g (½ cup) chopped
    sun-dried tomatoes
20–25 pitted kalamata
    olives, roughly chopped
250 ml (1 cup) beer,
    at room temperature

1   Put all the ingredients, except the beer, into a large bowl, preferably a metal one as it will need to sit by the heat at one point. Add about three-quarters of the beer and use your hands to bring the mixture together. If the dough seems too dry add a bit more beer, but don't add too much that the dough is sticky and difficult to handle. Knead in the bowl for about 10 minutes, or until soft and elastic.

2   Cover the dough with a clean tea towel and place close to the fire (but not on it) or in a warm place for 30 minutes, until the dough has risen in size. At the same time, place your camp oven close to the fire to warm through, but don't let it get too hot.

3   Transfer the dough to the camp oven, cover, and sit it close to the fire so it is surrounded by coals – you can put some coals on the lid as well. It's very important not to sit the camp oven on top of the coals as the bottom will burn. If cooking over a fire pit with a grill tray that swings round, put the camp oven on this and carefully put some coals on top of the camp oven too, to ensure an all-round heat.

4   Cook for 30–40 minutes, checking the coals every now and then, adding more as necessary, until the bread is cooked and it sounds hollow when tapped. If your bread is taking longer to cook, don't worry, just ensure you keep replacing the coals. Carefully remove from the camp oven, leave for 5 minutes, then serve in chunks or slices.

PAN BAGNAT

Pan bagnat is a traditional French recipe and is literally a baguette soaked lightly in olive oil and filled with delicious ingredients. The traditional recipe uses tuna as part of the filling, but you could replace it with chicken if preferred.

MAKES 1 long baguette

1 long bread stick
1 garlic clove, halved
60–80 ml (¼–½ cup)
   olive oil
3 firm, ripe tomatoes, sliced
1 small green capsicum
   (bell pepper), seeded
   and thinly sliced
15 pitted kalamata
   olives, halved
185 g (2–3 oz) can tuna in
   spring water, drained

1 Cut the bread stick in half horizontally and remove a little of the dough to form a hollow.

2 Rub the bread all over with the garlic halves, then liberally drizzle the olive oil all over the bread.

3 Layer the tomato, bell pepper, olives and tuna on one side of the baguette and season with salt and freshly ground black pepper. Top with the other baguette half.

4 Cut the filled baguette into four shorter lengths and wrap individually in foil or wax paper. Leave for at least an hour to allow the flavours to mingle and the oil to soak into the bread before serving.

Although tuna in oil could be used, it's easier and, in my opinion, better for the environment to drain spring water rather than oil at a campsite.

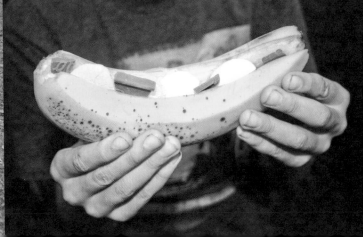

BALSAMIC ONION RELISH

This tasty onion relish works well served as an accompaniment to chargrilled steak and chicken, or is equally at home on cheese or chicken sandwiches. It is especially yummy with the pesto lamb burgers on page 58.

SERVES 4–6

- 2 large onions, halved and thinly sliced
- 1 tablespoon olive oil
- 1 tablespoon balsamic vinegar
- 2 teaspoons sugar

1 Put the onion in a bowl, add the oil and toss to coat. Place onto a hot campfire grill or in a frying pan over the fire or a gas cooker and cook for about 10 minutes, stirring regularly so they soften and turn golden brown but don't burn.

2 Scoop the onion into a pile, pour over the vinegar and sprinkle over the sugar. Mix together using a fork or tongs and cook for a further 2 minutes. Balsamic onion relish can be served warm or cool. Any leftovers can be covered and stored in the cooler for up to two days.

QUICK TOMATO SAUCE FOR PASTA

This is a useful sauce to prepare when you either don't have much time, or everything else has already been eaten. You can add chopped kalamata olives and fresh basil leaves or add some diced bell pepper and zucchini for a vegetable fix.

SERVES 4

- 1 tablespoon olive oil
- 1 large onion, halved and thinly sliced
- 2 garlic cloves, crushed
- 2 x 400 g (14 oz) can, diced tomatoes
- 2 teaspoons dried oregano
- 2 teaspoons sugar
- pasta, to serve
- grated cheese, to serve

1 Heat the olive oil in a heavy-based saucepan or large frying pan. Add the onion and garlic and cook for about 5 minutes over a gentle heat on a gas cooker or over a low fire.

2 Add the tomatoes, oregano and sugar and season well with salt and freshly ground black pepper. Cover and simmer for 10 minutes.

3 Cook the pasta according to the box instructions, serve with the sauce spooned over the top and sprinkle over some grated cheese.

Try adding 2 tablespoons of pesto and some chopped cooked sausages to the simmering sauce, or add a handful of chopped mushrooms with the onion and 125 ml (½ cup) of red wine with the tomatoes.

DELICIOUS ENDINGS

Although our meals often end with a square or two of chocolate when we are camping, there are a few tempting favourites that have stood the test of time. Bread and butter pudding in the fire is always well received and is a useful way of using up any leftover bread. Another decadent end to a meal involves wrapping a whole camembert or brie wheel in foil and sitting it on top of the fire until it melts and goes all gooey, then we dip bread and crackers into the melted cheese – memorable and delicious!

The kids love stuffing bananas with melted chocolate and marshmallows, then the whole family tucks in to enjoy the sweet delights. And finally, if you have a birthday to celebrate while you're camping, get yourself prepared and bake the coconut mini pavlovas before you go. They last much longer than a cake and you can top them with cream and fruit at the campsite before you serve them.

COCONUT PAVLOVAS

I am not suggesting you whip up a few mini pavlovas at the camp, but if you are celebrating a special occasion then a light, airy pavlova will last much longer than a traditional cake. Making individual pavlovas saves the mess of cutting. Make these the day before you go and store in an airtight container – they should last up to four days.

SERVES 6

3 egg whites
175 g (¾ cup) sugar
50 g (generous ½ cup)
  shredded coconut

TO SERVE

300 ml (10 oz) thickened
  (whipping) cream or a
  can of whipped cream
200 g (1⅓ cups) chopped
  strawberries
200 g (1⅓ cups) halved black
  and white seedless grapes
2 mangoes, peeled, pits
  removed and flesh diced

Don't forget the candles and a whisk for the cream.

1 Preheat the oven to 140°C (275°F/Gas 1). Grease and line two baking trays with parchment paper. Draw six circles, each with an 8 cm (3¼ in) diameter, onto the paper, then turn the paper over, ensuring you can still see the circles.

2 Put the egg whites in a clean, dry bowl and use electric beaters to whisk until soft peaks form. Add the sugar 1 heaped tablespoon at a time, and whisk until the mixture is stiff and glossy. Gently fold in the shredded coconut.

3 Spoon the egg white mixture onto the circles, using the back of a spoon to fill the circle shapes, but leaving them rough and ready with a few peaks, rather than with perfectly smooth tops and sides. Bake for 1 hour. Turn the oven off and leave for a further 1 hour – stick a wooden spoon in the oven door to hold it open and allow the pavlovas to finish cooking and dry out slightly.

4 Remove the pavlovas from the oven and transfer to wire racks to cool completely. Store in an airtight container between layers of parchment paper.

AT THE CAMP

5 If using whipping cream, put into a bowl and whisk until thickened. Top each pavlova with cream and then your choice of strawberries, grapes and mango. Decorate with candles if required.

BREAD AND BUTTER PUDDING IN THE FIRE

This is the perfect way to use up any leftover bread, as bits and pieces from different loaves can be used. If cream isn't available, use all milk instead. If a sweeter pudding is preferred, spread the bread with some jam when buttering. On a camping trip one Easter we used sliced, leftover hot cross buns and it was absolutely divine.

SERVES 4–6

softened butter, for spreading
8 slices of bread, halved
60 g (⅓ cup) raisins (optional)
3 eggs
3 tablespoons sugar
300 ml (1¼ cup) whipping cream (or an additional 300 ml/1¼ cup milk)
375 ml (1½ cups) milk

Don't forget a whisk and a dish to bake this in.

1 Lightly grease a camp oven or 2-litre (8-cup) capacity fire-proof dish with butter.

2 Spread each slice of bread with butter (and jam, if using) and arrange in the dish in layers from front to back so the slices are standing up against each other. Scatter over the raisins, if using.

3 Using a whisk or fork, whisk together the eggs, sugar, cream and milk until well combined. Slowly pour over the bread, letting the bread soak up the liquid a little. Set aside for 10 minutes to allow a little more soaking.

4 Put the lid on the camp oven or cover the dish with foil, then sit it on the edges of the fire surrounded by coals. Make sure there are no coals underneath the oven or it will burn the base. Leave for about 30 minutes, or until the custard has set. Alternatively, you can cook this pudding in a covered barbecue with only the outside burners turned on low.

5 Remove from the heat, spoon into bowls and serve immediately.

Don't forget the foil.

BAKED MELTED CHEESE

Cheese is a great way to end a meal, especially for those who don't have a sweet tooth. Baking a whole wheel of cheese over a fire until it is oozing and melted takes it to a whole new level – this is camping at its decadent best!

MAKES 1 cheese

1 whole brie or
   camembert wheel
crusty bread or
   crackers, to serve

1 Remove any wax wrapping from the cheese, reserving the wooden box if it has one.

2 Wrap the cheese in a double layer of foil. Place on a campfire grill or on the barbecue, or even into a frying pan over a gas cooker. Cook for 4–5 minutes on each side, or until the cheese feels really soft when pressed.

3 Carefully unwrap the cheese and either serve from the foil or return to the box. Cut a cross in the top to open it up and start dipping in pieces of crusty bread or crackers.

WARM SPICED WINE

Put someone in charge of making this wine while others prepare dinner or put the kids to bed. Then spend the evening huddled around the fire, sipping delicious warm spiced wine!

MAKES 1 bottle

750 ml (25 oz) bottle
   red wine, don't use
   your best bottle!
110 g (½ cup) sugar
2 oranges
8 cloves
1 cinnamon stick

1 Pour the wine into a large saucepan, add the sugar and stir to dissolve. Place over the fire while you prepare the oranges, but do not let the wine boil.

2 Stick the cloves into the skin of one of the oranges in a random pattern, then thickly slice the orange. Squeeze the juice from the second orange into the wine mixture, then add the orange slices to the pan with the cinnamon stick. Simmer gently for 30 minutes.

3 Let the spiced wine cool for 5 minutes, then pour into mugs.

BANANAS WITH MELTED CHOCOLATE AND MARSHMALLOWS

I've made this recipe to serve four people but you can make as many of these as you need, allowing for one banana per person. For extra decadence, adults can drizzle cream and a drop of rum over their cooked bananas, although they taste just as good without.

SERVES 4

4 bananas (skin on)
40 g (⅓ cup) milk chocolate, broken into pieces
12 marshmallows, halved

1 Use a sharp knife to carefully make a slit along the inner curve of each banana, cutting through the skin but ensuring you don't cut through the skin on the other side. Gently push the banana from either end to open up the middle of the banana – you should have a long wide slit to put your filling into.

2 Insert the chocolate pieces and marshmallows alternately into the slit in the middle of the banana to fill it up.

3 Wrap each banana in foil and place in the hot coals for about 15 minutes, turning occasionally, until the banana skins have gone black and mushy. Alternatively, you can wrap in foil and cook in a frying pan over a gas cooker for about 20 minutes, turning every 5 minutes or so.

4 Very carefully unwrap the bananas as they will be very hot. Serve with a spoon to scoop out the gooey insides.

If you don't have any chocolate, add a few teaspoons of Nutella instead.

CREAMY RICE PUDDING

This tasty dessert can be cooked over fire or a gas cooker. If cooking over a fire, ensure you stir it regularly to prevent the bottom burning. This recipe is a particular favourite of my friend and her children, who always request it whatever the weather! You can also use basmati rice, but it won't be quite as creamy.

SERVES 4

120 g (¾ cup) risotto rice
900 ml (3¾ cups) full-fat milk
60 g (⅓ cup) sugar
1 teaspoon salt
1 thick slice orange
　peel (optional)
soft brown sugar, to serve
raisins, to serve
strawberry jam, to serve

1　Put the rice, milk, sugar, salt and orange peel, if using, into a large heavy-based saucepan and stir well. Put the lid on.

2　If cooking over gas, bring to the boil, then reduce the heat and simmer gently for 30–40 minutes, stirring regularly and scraping the base of the pan to prevent the rice from sticking and burning. Cook until the rice is tender and most of the milk has been absorbed. You may need to add some extra milk if the rice isn't soft. Remove from the heat and give the rice pudding a really good stir.

3　If cooking over a fire, sit the pan on the swing arm over the fire and cook following the directions above. If cooking over coals, sit the pan close to the fire initially to bring to the boil (keeping a close eye on it), then remove to a much cooler part of the fire and gently simmer, replacing the coals as necessary. It will probably take more like 45–50 minutes to cook this way, but it will all depend on the heat of the coals. You may need to add extra milk if necessary.

4　Remove the orange peel (if using) and serve the rice pudding accompanied by raisins, brown sugar and jam, if desired.

INDEX

arugula *see* rocket

artichokes 97

aubergines *see* eggplant

avocado

    Green salad with lemon and mustard mayonnaise dressing 115

    Guacamole 139

    Pasta salad with bacon, avocado, rocket and cherry tomatoes 94

    Sweet chilli chicken baguettes 52

bacon

    Egg salad on crusty toasts 102

    Pasta salad with bacon, avocado, rocket and cherry tomatoes 94

    Spanish tortilla 60

    Warm tortilla roll-ups 125

baguettes *see* rolls/baguettes

Baked melted cheese 162

Balsamic onion relish 154

bananas

    Banana and coconut bread 2

    Bananas with melted chocolate and marshmallows 166

Barley 'risotto' with butternut squash 84

beans

    Easy fish and vegetable stew 43

    Hearty bean and vegetable soup 80

    One-pot lamb shoulder with white beans and tomato sauce 86

    Pasta, bean and vegetable stew 83

    Pesto fish with bean salad 42

    Tuna and bean salad 103

beef

    Beef kebabs 130

    Camp-made sausages 61

    Cheesy beef burgers 128

    Chilli beef and vegetables 22

    Kofta with yoghurt and pita bread 20

    Leftover fried-rice 75

    Meatballs in tomato sauce 28

    Spaghetti bolognaise chock-full of vegies 18

    Thai beef salad with noodles 104

Beer and pesto campfire bread damper 147

beetroot, Hearty sausage salad 100

bocconcini 112

bread (see also campfire bread*)*

    Banana and coconut bread 2

    Bread and butter pudding in the fire 160

    Egg salad on crusty toasts 102

    Kofta with yoghurt and pita bread 20

    pita bread 130

    Pita calzone pizzas 126

    Breakfast pancakes 124

cabbage, Fish fillets with crunchy Asian coleslaw 48

Cajun-marinated white fish fillets 31

campfire bread

    Beer and pesto campfire bread 147

    Cheese and herb campfire bread 146

    Kids' easy campfire bread 144

    Sundried tomato and olive campfire bread 148

Camp-made sausages 61

capers 96, 106

carrots

    Chicken and root vegetable stew 70

    Hearty bean and vegetable soup 80

    One-pot roast chicken with vegetables 78

    Pork and veal mince with root vegetables 30

    Roast pork with vegetables 82

    Spaghetti bolognaise chock-full of vegies 18

Chargrilled corn, tomato and radicchio salad 120

Chargrilled lamb with haloumi, olives and lemon 106

Chargrilled zucchini, onion and feta salad 110

cheese (see also bocconcini; feta)

Baked melted cheese 162

Cheese and ham tortilla triangles 134

Cheese and herb campfire bread damper 146

Cheesy beef burgers 128

Pita calzone pizzas 126

Warm tortilla roll-ups 125

chicken

Chicken kebabs 130

Chicken and root vegetable stew 70

One-pot roast chicken with vegetables 78

Pan bagnat 150

Simple chicken satay 132

Smoked chicken and potato salad with caper and mustard mayonnaise 96

Sweet chilli chicken baguettes 52

Sweet and spicy chicken pieces 54

Warm tortilla roll-ups 125

Yoghurt and spice marinated chicken 23

chickpeas

Chickpea, feta and tomato salad108

Vegetable and chickpea casserole 34

chilli

Chilli beef and vegetables 22

Sweet chilli chicken baguettes 52

Sweet and spicy chicken pieces 54

Thai beef salad with noodles 104

Vietnamese pork meatballs with noodles 56

chipolatas 138

chocolate

Bananas with melted chocolate and marshmallows 166

Chocolate brownies 14

Chocolate chip cookies 10

coconut

Banana and coconut bread 2

Coconut pavlovas 158

Colourful tomato and mozzarella salad with balsamic dressing 112

cookies

Chocolate chip cookies 10

Oat and raisin cookies 6

Wholemeal oatcakes 7

corn

Chargrilled corn, tomato and radicchio salad 120

Egg salad on crusty toasts 102

courgettes *see* zucchini

Crunchy romaine and radish salad 114

cucumbers

Chickpea, feta and tomato salad 108

Green salad with lemon and mustard mayonnaise dressing 115

Lemon, feta and tomato salad 118

Marinated pork loin with Greek salad 64

Thai beef salad with noodles 104

curry

Massaman lamb curry with potatoes 74

Quick mild fish curry 43

damper *see* campfire bread

dips, Peanut butter dip 139

dressings

balsamic chilli 94

lemon 92

lemon caper 102

lemon and herb 106

mustard mayonnaise 115

tangy 108

vinegar and herb 103

vinegar mayonnaise 100

vinegar mustard 114

dried fruit

Homemade fruit and nut muesli squares 4

Oat and raisin cookies 6

Easy fish and vegetable stew 46

Egg salad on crusty toasts 102

eggplant, Vegetable and chickpea casserole 34

fennel, Chicken and root vegetable stew 70

feta 64, 108, 110, 118

fish

Cajun-marinated white fish fillets 31

Easy fish and vegetable stew 46

Fish fillets with crunchy Asian coleslaw 48

Foil wrapped fillets of fish with tomatoes, olives and herbs 38

Marinated fish fillets 32

Pan bagnat 150

Pesto fish with bean salad 42

Quick fish kebabs 40

Quick mild fish curry 43

Soba noodle and smoked fish
salad 92

Tuna and bean salad 103

Flapjacks 14

Foil wrapped fillets of fish with
tomatoes, olives and herbs 38

grapes, Coconut pavlovas 158

Green salad with lemon
and mustard mayonnaise
dressing 115

guacamole 138

haloumi 106

ham

Cheese and ham tortilla
triangles 134

Warm tortilla roll-ups 125

harissa 20, 32

Hearty bean and vegetable soup 80

Hearty sausage salad 100

Homemade fruit and nut granola
bars 4

Honey and soy sausages 138

Kids' easy campfire damper 144

Kofta with yoghurt and pita
bread 20

lamb

Chargrilled lamb with haloumi,
olives and lemon 106

Kofta with yoghurt and pita
bread 20

Marinated butterflied leg of
lamb 55

Massaman lamb curry with
potatoes 74

One-pot lamb shoulder with white
beans and tomato sauce 86

Pesto lamb burgers 58

Leftover fried-rice 75

Lentil, feta and tomato salad 118

lettuce 52, 58, 61, 114, 115

mangetout *see* snow peas

Marinated butterflied leg of
lamb 55

Marinated fish fillets 32

Marinated pork loin with Greek
salad 64

marshmallows 166

Massaman lamb curry with
potatoes 74

mayonnaise 100, 115

caper and mustard 96

mustard and herb 66

Meatballs in tomato sauce 28

'Messy' platter 139

noodles

Soba noodle and smoked fish
salad 92

Thai beef salad with noodles 104

Vietnamese pork meatballs with
noodles 56

nuts

Chocolate brownies 15

Chocolate chip cookies 10

Homemade fruit and nut muesli
squares 4

Oat and raisin cookies 6

Oat and raisin cookies 6

olives

Chargrilled lamb with haloumi,
olives and lemon 106

Foil wrapped fillets of fish with
tomatoes, olives and herbs 38

Marinated pork loin with Greek
salad 64

One-pot lamb shoulder with white
beans and tomato sauce 86

Pan bagnat 150

Sundried tomato and olive
campfire bread damper 148

One-pot lamb shoulder with white
beans and tomato sauce 86

One-pot roast chicken with
vegetables 78

onions

Balsamic onion relish 154

Chargrilled zucchini, onion and
feta salad 110

Pan bagnat 150

pancakes, Breakfast pancakes 124

parsnips, Pork and veal mince with
root vegetables 30

pasta

Meatballs in tomato sauce 28

Pasta, bean and vegetable stew 83

Pasta salad with bacon, avocado, arugula, cherry tomatoes 94

Pasta salad with roasted vegetables 97

Spaghetti bolognaise chock-full of vegies 18

pavlova, Coconut pavlovas 158

Pear and raspberry loaf 12

peas

Barley 'risotto' with pumpkin 84

Pot-roasted pork with potatoes and peas 88

pesto 83

Beer and pesto campfire bread damper 147

Pasta salad with roasted vegetables 97

Pesto fish with bean salad 42

Pesto lamb burgers 58

pine nuts 92

Pita calzone pizzas 126

pizza, Pita calzone pizzas 126

pork

Camp-made sausages 61

Marinated pork loin with Greek salad 64

Meatballs in tomato sauce 28

Pork kebabs with flavoured mayonnaise 66

Pork and veal mince with root vegetables 30

Pot-roasted pork with potatoes and peas 88

Roast pork with vegetables 82

Teriyaki marinated pork 26

Vietnamese pork meatballs with noodles 56

Pot-roasted pork with potatoes and peas 88

potatoes

Easy fish and vegetable stew 43

Hearty bean and vegetable soup 80

Hearty sausage salad 100

Massaman lamb curry with potatoes 74

One-pot roast chicken with vegetables 78

Pot-roasted pork with potatoes and peas 88

Roast pork with vegetables 82

Smoked chicken and potato salad with caper and mustard mayonnaise 96

Spanish tortilla 60

pumpkin

Barley 'risotto' with pumpkin 84

Chicken and root vegetable stew 70

Queso blanco *see* haloumi

Quick fish kebabs 40

Quick mild fish curry 43

Quick tomato sauce for pasta 154

radicchio, Chargrilled corn, tomato and radicchio salad 120

radishes, Crunchy romaine and radish salad 114

raspberries, Pear and raspberry loaf 12

rice

Creamy rice pudding 167

Leftover fried-rice 75

Roast pork with vegetables 82

rocket 42, 52, 61, 94, 106, 115

rolled oats

Flapjacks 14

Homemade fruit and nut muesli squares 4

Oat and raisin cookies 6

Wholemeal biscuits 7

rolls/baguettes

Camp-made sausages 61

Cheesy beef burgers 128

Pan bagnat 150

Pesto lamb burgers 58

Sweet chilli chicken baguettes 52

salads

Chargrilled corn, tomato and radicchio salad 120

Chargrilled lamb with haloumi, olives and lemon 106

Chargrilled zucchini, onion and feta salad 110

Chickpea, feta and tomato salad 108

Colourful tomato and bocconcini salad with balsamic dressing 112

Crunchy romaine and radish salad 114

Egg salad on crusty toasts 102

Green salad with lemon and mustard mayonnaise dressing 115

Hearty sausage salad 100

Lentil, feta and tomato salad 118

Marinated pork loin with Greek salad 64

Pasta salad with bacon, avocado, rocket and cherry tomatoes 94

Pasta salad with roasted vegetables 97

Pesto fish with bean salad 42

Smoked chicken and potato salad with caper and mustard mayonnaise 96

Soba noodle and smoked fish
salad 92

Thai beef salad with noodles
104

Tuna and bean salad 103

sauces/relishes

Balsamic onion relish 154

Quick tomato sauce for
pasta 154

sausages

Camp-made sausages 61

Hearty sausage salad 100

Honey and soy sausages 138

'Messy' platter 139

Simple chicken satay 132

Smoked chicken and potato
salad with caper and mustard
mayonnaise 96

snow peas

Fish fillets with crunchy Asian
coleslaw 48

Quick mild fish curry 43

Soba noodle and smoked fish
salad 92

soup, Hearty bean and vegetable
soup 80

Spaghetti bolognaise chock-full of
vegies 18

Spanish tortilla 60

strawberries, Coconut pavlovas 158

Sundried tomato and olive campfire
bread damper 148

Sweet chilli chicken baguettes 52

Sweet and spicy chicken pieces 54

Teriyaki marinated pork 26

Thai beef salad with noodles 104

tomatoes/tomato sauce

Chargrilled corn, tomato and
radicchio salad 120

Chickpea, feta and tomato salad
108

Chilli beef and vegetables 22

Colourful tomato and bocconcini
salad with balsamic dressing
112

Easy fish and vegetable stew 46

Foil wrapped fillets of fish with
tomatoes, olives, herbs 38

Hearty bean and vegetable
soup 80

Lentil, feta and tomato salad 118

Meatballs in tomato sauce 28

One-pot lamb shoulder with white
beans and tomato sauce 86

Pita calzone pizzas 126

Pork and veal mince with root
vegetables 30

Quick tomato sauce for
pasta 154

Sundried tomato and olive
campfire bread damper 148

Thai beef salad with noodles 104

tortillas

Cheese and ham tortilla
triangles 134

Warm tortilla roll-ups 125

Tuna and bean salad 103

veal, Pork and veal mince with root
vegetables 30

Vegetable and chickpea
casserole 34

Vietnamese pork meatballs with
noodles 56

Warm spiced wine 162

Warm tortilla roll-ups 125

Wholemeal biscuits 7

wine, Warm spiced wine 162

winter squash *see* pumpkin

yoghurt

Kofta with yoghurt and pita
bread 20

Yoghurt and spice marinated
chicken 23

zucchini

Chargrilled zucchini, onion and
feta salad 110

Chilli beef and vegetables 22

Pasta, bean and vegetable
stew 83

Pasta salad with roasted
vegetables 97

Quick fish kebabs 40

Spaghetti bolognaise chock-full
of vegies 18

Vegetable and chickpea
casserole 34

AUTHOR'S ACKNOWLEDGEMENTS

I have loved every minute of putting this book together, but it was definitely a team effort. Firstly, I cannot thank my amazing photography team enough. Tash – you were rarely without your camera, capturing life around the campsite as it unfolded, producing images I had so hoped for. Grace – your cooking and chopping never faltered, even when you were stalked numerous times by a large monitor lizard! Maria – your fire building skills are now legendary – thanks for all of your help and support.

Thanks to my publisher, Melissa Kayser, who remained calm at all times and who from the beginning was as excited about this book as I was. Thanks to Erika Budiman, who conceived the fabulous design for the book and to Jacqueline Blanchard, my editor, who crafted the recipes and ramblings to fit the page.

I must say a big thank you to all my gorgeous models, Max, Jack, Dylan, Liam, Mia, Chante, Jess, Lulu, Findlay, Molly and Hugo. Special thanks must also go to our regular camping companions, Charlie and Illya, who initially put the idea for this book into my head. You were right, it's time to show fellow campers that good food isn't hard to create while camping.

Thank you to my husband, Alex, who very happily spends his life trying new recipe ideas, whether it's around the dinner table at home, the fire-pit in our garden, or a campfire in the middle of the bush.

Finally, a massive thank you to my mum and dad for taking us on numerous camping trips to France where my love of camping was born. Mum – thank you for introducing me to a variety of weird and wonderful food from an early age and nurturing our family with so many delicious meals.

PUBLISHER'S ACKNOWLEDGEMENTS

This edition published in 2017 by Hardie Grant Books, an imprint of Hardie Grant Publishing. First published in 2013.

COMMISSIONING EDITOR
Melissa Kayser

MANAGING EDITOR
Marg Bowman

PROJECT MANAGER AND EDITOR
Jacqueline Blanchard, Kate J Armstrong

EDITORIAL ASSISTANT
Alison Proietto, Jamie Birdwell

DESIGN AND LAYOUT
Erika Budiman

PHOTOGRAPHY
Natasha Milne

HOME ECONOMIST
Grace Campbell

ASSISTANT HOME ECONOMIST
Maria Madill

INDEX
Max McMaster

TYPESETTER
Megan Ellis

PRE-PRESS
Megan Ellis, Splitting Image Colour Studio

Thanks to Anaconda, Spotlight and Sunny Jim for supplying props for use at the photo shoot.

Note on measurements: This book uses metric cup measurements, i.e. 250 ml for 1 cup; in the US a cup is 8 fl oz, just smaller, and American cooks should be generous in their cup measurements. This book also uses 15 ml (½ fl oz) tablespoons; cooks with 20 ml (¾ fl oz) tablespoons should be scant with their tablespoon measurements.

Hardie Grant Books (Melbourne)
Building 1, 658 Church Street
Richmond, Victoria 3121
hardiegrantbooks.com.au

Hardie Grant Books (London)
5th & 6th Floors
52-54 Southwark Street
London SE1 1UN
Hardiegrantbooks.co.uk

A Cataloguing-in-Publication entry is available from the catalogue of the National Library of Australia at www.nla.gov.au

US ISBN 9781741176230

10 9 8 7 6 5 4 3 2 1

Printed in China by 1010 Printing International Ltd